HOW TO (ALMOST) MAKE FRIENDS ON THE INTERNET

HOW TO (ALMOST) MAKE FRIENDS ON THE INTERNET

MICHAEL CUNNINGHAM

First published in Great Britain in 2020 by Trapeze
an imprint of The Orion Publishing Group Ltd
Carmelite House, 50 Victoria Embankment
London EC4Y 0DZ

An Hachette UK Company

1 3 5 7 9 10 8 6 4 2

A CIP catalogue record for this book is
available from the British Library.

ISBN (Hardback) 978 1 3987 0181 6
ISBN (eBook) 978 1 3987 0182 3

Typeset by seagulls.net
Printed and bound in great Britain by Clays Ltd, Elcograf S.p.A.

MIX
Paper from
responsible sources
FSC
www.fsc.org   FSC® C104740

www.orionbooks.co.uk

This book is dedicated to Padraig, Marian, Olivia, Justin, Holly, Jack and Sam, my top 7 favourite people. But this top 7 is not set in stone so don't get complacent.

This book is absolutely NOT dedicated to everyone who has ever wronged me (and there are a lot of you). I keep a running tally of personal grievances so don't think that I've forgotten any injustices that have been visited upon me. If you have seen the error of your ways and now wish to apologise for wronging me, please email your admission of wrongdoing to iwrongedyoumichael@gmail.com and I will consider your punishment.

Contents

●●●

PART II – PLEASURE

Intro

Hi. I am Michael. When I was first contacted by a publisher about publishing a collection of my communications with the world as a book, my first reaction was: 'About time. Finally, after years of books about wizards and dragons, they've come to their senses and contacted a serious person for a serious book.'

Today's modern world offers limitless opportunities to form new friendships, which most people are not tech-savvy enough to make best use of. And while obviously not everyone can be an online people person/business tycoon like me, don't worry, because most of what I am about to teach you is applicable to everyone.

All you're going to need is an internet connection, an open mind, unshakeable self-belief and unrestricted access to a printer that someone else pays for.

Don't be afraid if the road ahead gets a little bumpy. Don't be dissuaded by people getting mad at you or questioning your ideas or calling you an idiot. All of history's great visionaries were doubted initially. By the end of this journey, you will have learned how to do the most important things in the world: how to make friends and be a respected member of both the online and your local community.

And if you think it sounds like my methods are an inefficient way of making friends, I advise you to check out a documentary called *You've Got Mail* whose synopsis I once read on Wikipedia, which conclusively proves that disputes and anger are often just a precursor to finding love and companionship.

Part I

Business

Entrepreneurship

Statistically, successful people have more friends than unsuccessful people. I am not sure if that is a real statistic or one I just thought of, but it's the reason why I start lots of small businesses and side careers. After all, the more successful businesses I am involved with, the more friendships I'm likely to form.

Buy and Sell

Elizabeth: 12:52

Elizabeth: 12:53

Anyone interested in this stereo and speakers? Very good condition. Works perfectly. Looking for €30. Thanks.

Luke: 12:56

Speaker on the right looks damaged

Elizabeth: 12:59

That's why I said very good condition, not excellent. Only minor damage and didn't affect sound.

Elizabeth: 12:59

Doesn't affect sound

Michael: 13:03

Is the blue bucket included?

Elizabeth: 13:04

Haha if you want it.

Michael: 13:05

Can I buy it without the stereo and speakers?

Elizabeth: 13:05

How much?

Michael: 13:07

€1. That is my final offer. Unless you reject it, in which case I will immediately return with an improved offer.

Elizabeth: 13:07

No, not worth the effort for €1, sorry.

Michael: 13:08

€1.01. That is my final offer. Unless you reject it, in which case I will immediately return with an improved offer.

Elizabeth: 13:08

No.

Michael: 13:09

€1.02. That is my final offer. Unless you reject it, in which case I will immediately return with an improved offer.

Elizabeth: 13:10

No, not selling to you now so don't bother bidding again. We don't do 1c increases here. Respect sellers please.

Daniel: 13:12

I'll offer a tenner for stereo/speakers Elizabeth if your looking for a start bid

Elizabeth: 13:13

Thanks Dan. Hoping to get more because it really is in good condition but will keep that in mind 🙏

Daniel: 13:17

No bother

Michael: 13:18

[Private Message to Daniel] Hi Dan. Michael here. Could you increase your offer for Elizabeth's stereo and speakers to €11.02 if she includes the blue bucket? Once the sale goes through, I will then give you the €1.02 for the bucket. Don't tell Elizabeth it's for me, though. Thanks 👍

Elizabeth: 13:19

I told you I'm not selling to you.
Take a hint.

Michael: 13:20

Please don't read my private
messages.

Elizabeth: 13:21

You posted it to the group, genius!!!

Michael: 13:26

Hi all. Am selling this blue bucket
if anyone wants to buy it. One
previous mean owner. Bids start at
€1.03

Elizabeth: 13:28

That's my bucket. Picture is cropped from mine.

Michael: 13:29

No, it's not. It's a bucket I bought from Dan. You interested?

Elizabeth: 13:32

Can one of the admins deal with this? That's cropped from my image. He doesn't own it. Not a real item.

Michael: 13:32

You can buy it from me for €1.03

Elizabeth: 13:33

I already own it.

Michael: 13:34

That's the spirit! Sold! Please paypal me the €1.03 at your earliest convenience. I'll deliver it later.

> **Michael: 13:34**
>
> Will leave it to the left of your stereo and speakers 👍

> **Michael: 13:34**
>
> Right, now that I've made a profit, I'm out of here. So long, suckers!

<You left>

You can't send messages to this group because you're no longer a participant.

Union Jack Bunting

Some people say that business and friendship don't mix. These people lack imagination and ambition. I have interjected myself into thousands of business dealings over the years and by doing so I have made almost several friends. When a commercial opportunity presents itself, seize it, sure, but don't forget to also use it as a way of building the foundations of a new friendship.

 John ▇▇▇▇▇▇ · 5 hrs

Looking to buy or borrow some union jack bunting as soon as possible if anyone has any.Need it before Friday. Reply or PM.

2 likes   53 comments 6 shares

 **Michael** · 2h

Hi John. Think maybe my uncle has some in his shed 👍

 **John** ▇▇▇▇▇▇ · 2h

Michael do you know what length? Is he selling or is he be willing to let me have it?

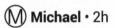 **Michael** · 2h

Will check with him now

 **John** ▇▇▇▇▇▇ · 2h

Thanks mate. Send a PM if you want.

Michael · 2h

I was going to call him. Not sure if he reads his private messages?

 **John** ▇▇▇▇▇▇ · 2h

No I mean PM me

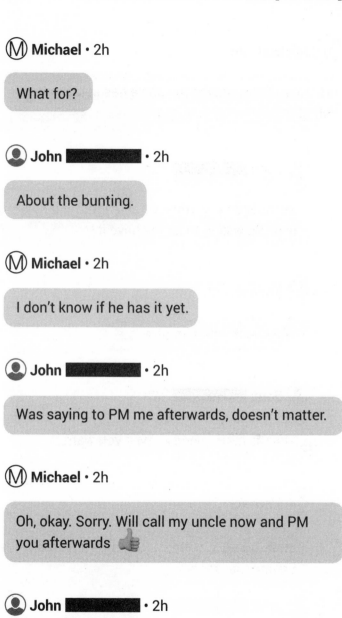

Michael · 2h

What for?

John ▮▮▮▮▮ · 2h

About the bunting.

Michael · 2h

I don't know if he has it yet.

John ▮▮▮▮▮ · 2h

Was saying to PM me afterwards, doesn't matter.

Michael · 2h

Oh, okay. Sorry. Will call my uncle now and PM you afterwards 👍

John ▮▮▮▮▮ · 2h

Nice one thanks.

Ⓜ Michael · 1h

Hi John. Just spoke with my uncle about the bunting. How do I send you a private message?

Ⓙ John ▪▪▪▪▪▪▪ · 52m

Go to my profile and click message. Cheers.

Ⓜ Michael · 44m

Okay, I've done that 👍

Ⓙ John ▪▪▪▪▪▪▪ · 38m

Haven't got it. Can you try again?

Ⓜ Michael · 37m

Okay 👍

Ⓙ John ▪▪▪▪▪▪▪ · 26m

Did you do it?

John  · 26m

I haven't got any messages from you.

Michael · 24m

I went to your profile and I clicked on 'Message' like you said and it brings up a form with your name at the top and an empty box underneath?

John  · 22m

Yeah, that's where you write the message.

Michael · 21m

Ah, okay. Now I'm with you. Will write it now

John  · 21m

Cheers

Michael · 17m

All done now 👍

 **John** ▮▮▮▮▮ · 14m

Still nothing on my end

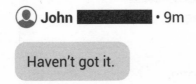 **Michael** · 12m

That's weird. I went to your profile, I clicked on 'Message' and I wrote the message in the box underneath your name?

 **John** ▮▮▮▮▮ · 9m

Haven't got it.

Michael · 7m

Am I supposed to click the 'Send' button underneath the message?

 **John** ▮▮▮▮▮ · 6m

Yes

 **Michael** · 4m

> Ah, now I see where I was going wrong. Hopefully
> this will do the trick

———————— [Facebook private message] ————————

John
You and John aren't connected on Facebook
Studied in ████████████████████████████
Lives in ███████████████

3:11pm

> Hi John,
>
> No, my uncle doesn't have any
> bunting in his shed.
>
> Michael

Haircut

Don't be afraid to look at things from new angles and disrupt traditional business models. After all, Steve Jobs didn't just stay making apples, he diversified into doing glitzy presentations about smart telephones.

FREE HAIRCUT!

Haircuts are becoming increasingly expensive. If you are interested in potentially getting a free haircut, *text the number below to find out more about this amazing opportunity!*

Michael

086 807 086 807 086 807 086 807 086 807 086 807 086 807 086 807 086 807 086 807 086 807 086 807 086 807 086 807

16:13

What's the story with getting a free haircut? Have I got the right number?

Michael *16:43*

Yes, this is the right number. Do you need a haircut now?

 16:46

No, but will need one in a few weeks tho. You a hairdresser?

Michael *16:48*

No but I have devised a way that we can both get free haircuts. It's risky but if we do this right, I think it will work

 16:49

What would I need to do? Explain it

Michael *16:51*

Okay, you know the barber shop on Barrack Street?

 16:52

Don't think so but I can find it.

Michael *16:57*

Okay, we'll meet there exactly 3 weeks from today. I'll get my hair cut first. Then, when it's finished and I'm about to pay, you stand up and say to the barber, 'Actually, this is my best friend Michael and I'll pay for both of us after I've got my haircut.'

Michael *16:58*

The barber will say, 'OK, that's fine.' I will then leave.

 17:01

Sorry, am stopping you there. Am not interested. I don't know you so I'm not paying for your haircut. No offence. Good luck.

Michael *17:02*

No, don't worry. You won't have to pay anything. That's just the beginning of the plan.

 17:03

Oh okay. Whats the rest of it?

Michael *17:17*

You will then get your hair cut as planned. But while you're getting your hair cut, I will have gone outside and put on a disguise (wig, glasses and fake moustache). Here's a diagram of what that will look like:

17:21

What is the plan? I thought you were giving free haircuts. Clearly not.

Michael *17:23*

Thanks to my disguise, it will be impossible for the barber to recognise me. I will then rejoin the queue and wait for you to finish getting your haircut.

Michael *17:25*

Then, when you are about to pay for it, I will stand up and say, 'Actually, this is my best friend Brian and I'll pay for both of us AND for the guy who was in here earlier.' The barber will say, 'Ok, that's fine.' You will then leave.

Michael *17:28*

I will then get ANOTHER haircut (don't worry, the barber will only be trimming the wig I'm wearing so it won't affect my earlier haircut). Meanwhile, after you've gone outside, you will find another disguise that I've hidden inside a green rucksack. You will then put it on and rejoin the queue.

Michael *17:31*

Then, when my haircut is finished and I'm about to pay, you will stand up and say, 'Actually, this is my best friend Simon and I'll pay for both of us AND for the two guys who were here earlier.'

Michael *17:32*

Hopefully if we keep doing this for long enough, the barber will lose track and forget to charge us for our original haircuts.

 17:34

Count me out. Thought you were offering a free haircut. Not interested in this stupid plan.

Michael *17:37*

Okay, what about if we just cut each other's hair? Do you have some scissors we could use?

25

Maths Tutorial

Don't forget to give feedback on other people's businesses. A lot of business people are too shy to ask for constructive criticism but that doesn't mean they don't want it. I find that, whatever the product or service, business people online are always happy to hear from me. By putting yourself out there like I do, you can almost make friends online every day.

 **Daniel** ▮▮▮▮▮▮▮▮▮ • 3 hrs

My wife and I are offering maths tutorials via video link so if any parents out there want to arrange tuition for their kids to keep them up to speed for when they go back to school, feel free to get in touch.

£20 per hour. Call anytime on ▮▮▮▮▮▮▮▮▮▮ or email us at ▮▮▮▮▮▮▮▮@gmail.com

2 likes   5 comments

 **Michael** · 19m

My uncle used to be a teacher and he always says that the one thing that can't be taught is maths. You've either got a mathematical brain or you don't. It's not something that people can learn.

Daniel  · 13m

With respect, Michael, that's completely wrong. I've taught maths for over fifteen years and I've seen the effects that teaching has. It absolutely *is* something people can learn.

Michael · 10m

Well, my uncle taught maths for over sixteen years so I think I'll take his word over a novice like you 👍

Daniel · 4m

I don't care if you believe me or not. I'm just telling you you're wrong. Of course maths can be taught. That's why we have maths classes in every school

(M) **Michael** · 1m

Tell that to my uncle. None of his students got any better at maths under his tutelage and most of them failed their exams miserably.

Pet-walking

What is the key to success in business?
Many people say it's cashflow. Others say it's developing the right product or service at the right time. And then there are people like me who say it's neither because the correct answer is clearly a pet-walking service that dares to be different.

FREE PET-WALKING SERVICE!

Are you pushed for time but want your pet to get more exercise?

Try our pet-walking service!

Your pet will be taken for a daily walk by one of our fully trained professionals.

Completely free for the first month! No obligation to continue afterwards!

Simply text the word "Walk" to the number below to get in touch!

086 807 086 807 086 807 086 807 086 807 086 807 086 807 086 807 086 807 086 807 086 807 086 807 086 807

16:06

WALK

Michael *16:10*

Hi. Thank you for expressing interest in our pet-walking service. Please answer the following questions to arrange your free trial.

Michael *16:10*

When would you like your pet to be taken for his/her walks?
-Mornings
-Afternoons
-Evenings

 16:11

Mornings

Michael *16:12*

Great! What type of pet would you like us to walk for you?
-Cat
-Horse
-Goat
-Other (please state)

16:14

Other (dog)

Michael *16:15*

Unfortunately our system does not recognise the animal you have chosen. Please re-enter the type of pet you would like to be walked, ensuring that the spelling is correct.

 16:15

Dog

Michael *16:16*

Unfortunately our system does not recognise the animal you have chosen. To speak with one of our operatives, please enter 1.

 16:17

1

Michael *16:20*

Hi. My name is Michael. How can I help?

16:22

I'm trying to sort out a free trial but it says it doesn't recognise the animal I picked. It's a dog

Michael *16:30*

Sorry about that. Just checked with my manager and our system was designed several years ago so it doesn't recognise newer words like 'dog'. What you and I call 'dogs' today are still listed in our database as 'domesticated wolves'.

Michael *16:30*

So when it asked you to choose your animal, you should have written 'domesticated wolf', or 'D-Wolf' for short.

 16:33

How was I supposed to know that? Would like to arrange it for mornings, Mon - Thursdays. Confirm first month is free yeah?

Michael *16:34*

First month is free, yes, but I can't take bookings, unfortunately. I haven't received the necessary training yet. I'm going to send you the automated message again. As long as you write D-Wolf, you shouldn't have any problems.

Michael *16:35*

What type of pet would you like us to walk for you?
-Cat
-Horse
-Goat
-Other (please state)

 16:36

D-Wolf

Michael *16:40*

You have chosen D-Wolf. We have consulted with our pet-walkers and asked if any of them would be willing to walk a D-Wolf. Unfortunately none of them have ever heard of a D-Wolf and they are not prepared to be in close proximity to one.

Michael *16:40*

If you would like us to walk a less scary-sounding pet, please write the animal type below.

 16:42

Should've known. F█████ing d-wolf. Jesus Christ

Michael *16:44*

Our system does not recognise the animal you have chosen. Please re-enter it below ensuring you have spelled it correctly (please note that we cannot accept bookings to walk D-Wolves at this time).

Campervan

· ·

Always be alert in business. What may be junk
to one person could be treasure to another.
Be alive to every opportunity.

· ·

(•) **Oliver**  · 3 hrs

Campervan wanted for upcoming season. Pref 5 or 6 berth. May consider one in need of repair. PM or reply below.

20 likes   11 comments

 **Michael** · 43m

Hi Oliver. Inherited a campervan from my grandad but I don't have a licence to drive it so I am not getting full value from it. Would consider serious offers.

 **Oliver** ▨▨▨▨ · 34m

Hi Michael. What sort of campervan is it?

 **Michael** · 23m

Not sure of the make and model. Don't really know much about this sort of thing and would be glad to have someone take it off my hands.

 **Oliver** ▨▨▨▨ · 20m

No probs, will PM you

———————— [Facebook private message] ————————

Oliver ▉▉▉▉
You and Oliver aren't connected on Facebook
Studied in ▉▉▉▉▉▉▉▉▉▉▉▉▉▉▉▉▉
Lives in ▉▉▉▉▉▉▉▉▉▉▉

Oliver ▉▉▉▉ · 18m

> Hi Michael. Sounds like unfortunately not getting best use of the campervan you inherited so hope we can do business. If you could find out make and model and is it CVRT'd that would be great. Thanks.

Michael · 17m

> Okay, will ask my grandmother when she gets back. She'll probably know.

Oliver ▉▉▉▉ · 16m

> Do you know what year it is?

Michael · 16m

> 2020

Oliver ▮▮▮▮▮ · 15m

It's brand new?

Michael · 15m

What is?

Oliver ▮▮▮▮▮ · 14m

Campervan?

Michael · 14m

Sorry, no, I thought you were asking what year is it now.

Oliver ▮▮▮▮▮ · 14m

No probs. I should have been clearer. How old is the campervan? Which year was it registered? Should be able to tell from the first 2 or 3 numbers on the number plate.

Michael · 13m

2014

Oliver ▮▮▮▮▮ · 12m

Brilliant. You got pics?

Michael · 10m

Not really. I've always had quite a slim build so I prefer to focus on speed training instead of trying to make my chest too muscular

Oliver ▮▮▮▮ · 10m

?

Michael · 10m

?

Oliver ▮▮▮ · 9m

What do you mean? Pics as in short for pictures.

Oliver ▮▮▮ · 9m

Are you talking about pecs?

Michael · 8m

Oh, sorry. That makes more sense. Was wondering why you were asking that.

Oliver ▐▬▬▬▌ • 5m

Can you send me some photos? Just want to get a look at it. What county you in? I live in ▐▬▬▬▌ but can travel if it's what I'm looking for and with in budget.

Michael • 5m

To be honest, I wouldn't really feel comfortable sending you photos of my chest. It's just that I'm a bit self-conscious about it and we don't really know each other very well yet.

Oliver ▐▬▬▬▌ • 4m

Very good. No way are you for real. Not a f▐▬▌ing chance. Bailing out now before I waste any more time. Good luck.

Family Portraits

For too long, the family portrait industry has been held back by an old-fashioned and overly reactive business model. Don't wait for customers to come to you. Get out there and find some clients/friends before one of your competitors does.

FREE FAMILY PORTRAIT!

Ever wanted a beautiful portrait of you and your family?

Created by a professional artist free of charge!

No family too big or too small!

All inquiries welcome!

Simply text the word "Portrait" to the number below to get in touch!

086 807 086 807 086 807 086 807 086 807 086 807 086 807 086 807 086 807 086 807 086 807 086 807 086 80

13:08

Portrait

Michael *13:31*

Hi! You have expressed interest in being the subject of a family portrait. Please confirm you are at least 18 years of age and please advise on the number of people you wish to be included in the portrait.

 13:32

Much older unfortunately

 13:33

4. Me, my wife and 2 sons.

Michael *13:33*

Thank you. Your artist will be in contact shortly

 13:34

OK 👍

Michael *14:18*

Hi there. My name is Michael and I'll be the artist for your family portrait. First of all, though, I just need some information on what type of portrait you're looking for.

 14:19

OK. Just checking this is all free is it?

Michael *14:21*

Yes. Don't worry. It's completely free. Hopefully you'll spread the word about it afterwards, though, and I'll be able to get more clients.

 14:22

No problem

 14:22

What info do you need?

Michael *14:24*

Would you like your portrait to be in an indoor or outdoor setting?

 14:26

I don't mind. Outdoors if its all the same to you

Michael *14:27*

Excellent choice. And do you want it to be formal or informal?

 14:28

Informal 👌

Michael *14:29*

Perfect. I'll be in touch.

 14:29

Michael *16:45*

Hi again. Are you ready for your free family portrait?

16:51

Yeah lets arrange a time, weekends are best for us. When suits you?

Michael *16:52*

 16:53

Whats this?

Michael *16:55*

That's your family portrait, silly! I hope you like it. I didn't know what you all look like so I had to guess. Hopefully I got it right.

Michael *16:55*

Also, I don't know if you have any pets so I drew a horse.

16:57

I thought you said your an artist?

Michael *17:05*

Do you not like it? Is it the horse? If you want, I can erase that horse and draw a slightly smaller horse instead?

Michael *19:16*

Hi. Michael again from earlier. I sensed you were disappointed with your portrait so I've tried to make it more exciting. I've drawn a picture of me jumping off the horse while doing karate! OMG, can you imagine that happening?! Hopefully you'll like this one more!

Michael *19:16*

19:18

Thanks

Michael *19:20*

You're welcome. I've already framed it and now it's hanging up in my kitchen. It'll always remind me of the day you and I became friends.

Michael *19:28*

Hey. I'm not busy for the rest of the week if you want to hang out? We could go to the cinema or just watch TV or whatever, I don't mind. We don't have to, though. It's just an idea. Let me know.

Waspkeeper

For too long 'keeping' has been connected to just one sort of buzzing insect. This failure of imagination leaves open a huge gap in the market for a dynamic new entrant who dares to be different.

 Jonathan ▓▓▓▓▓▓ • 6 hrs

***IMPORTANT

Hey all. I've been told there's a small wasps nest to the left of the front entrance. We don't think it's in use but to be on the safe side, please keep all windows shut and use the door at the back of the building until further notice when entering or leaving the building.

61 comments

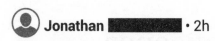 **Jonathan** ▮▮▮▮▮▮▮ • 2h

***Update
Spoke to pest control about the wasp nest and they'll be here tomorrow afternoon. Until then continue to keep windows shut and use the back door when entering or leaving the building. Thanks for your cooperation.

 **Michael** • 2h

Not until tomorrow? My uncle is a waspkeeper so I could ask him to take care of it today?

 **Gav** ▮▮▮▮▮ • 2h

is a wasp keeper a real thing?

Michael • 2h

Yes, Gav. It might not require a business suit or a fancy college degree but it's an honest profession that deserves respect

Gav ▮▮▮▮▮ • 2h

cool, just neverheard of it

Ⓜ **Michael** · 2h

If **Jonathan** hires him, you could get to meet him and maybe apologise for insinuating that he doesn't have a real job? 👍

👤 **Jonathan** ▮▮▮▮▮▮ · 2h

Michael. Thanks, I got it all arranged now but thanks for the offer.

Ⓜ **Michael** · 1h

Hi Jonathan. Thanks for getting back to me. Spoke with my uncle a couple of minutes ago and told him you had hired someone to deal with it tomorrow. He said that if you had hired him, he would have dealt with it today 👍

👤 **Jonathan** ▮▮▮▮▮▮ · 1h

Thanks. Hopefully this will sort it out and will be back to normal tomorrow.

Ⓜ **Michael** · 1h

My uncle would probably have done it for cheaper too. His prices are the best in town 👍

Jonathan ▆▆▆▆▆▆▆ • 1h

It's done now mate so let it go.

Michael • 58m

Just saying that if you had consulted with me beforehand, we could have dealt with the issue quicker and for a lower price and then split the remainder between us 👍

Jonathan ▆▆▆▆▆▆▆ • 57m

Okay you've made your point now, well done, good job.

Michael • 52m

I know but it's just something to bear in mind if this ever happens again, which it easily could because my uncle says there must have been something about that spot to attract wasps in the first place. Can give you his number if you want to call him for advice or a chat?

Wayne  • 43m

For f█████s sake man John already told you he was dealing with it, no need to go on about it for like 30 posts.

Michael • 40m

Sorry for taking wasp safety procedures seriously. Didn't realise that was a crime around here.

Wayne ████████ • 37m

Don't get sarcastic with me, you just got to learn when to drop it

Michael • 32m

I'll drop it when there are ZERO global deaths per annum from wasp-related injuries instead of the current 27*

*as per 2019 World Health Organisation figures

 **Michael** · 25m

Also, just want to mention that my uncle offered some expert advice for how residents should deal with the situation until the nest is removed if anyone is interested?

Michael · 15m

Haven't seen any replies to my previous message so it must not have gone through but basically my uncle, in his professional capacity, advises that residents keep their windows shut and use the entrance to the rear of the building until the matter is resolved 👍

 **Wayne** ▆▆▆▆▆▆ · 12m

Read first post. John already said that

Michael · 8m

No offence to Jonathan, who seems like a semi-competent person trying his best in this wasp crisis, but residents are more likely to follow advice that they know has come from a professional waspkeeper 👍

Jonathan  • 7m

What apartment are you in? Do you even live in the building?

Michael • 4m

Am quite a private person so would prefer not to answer that, thanks 👍

Elaine  • 3m

Meaning he doesn't live here 😂

Michael • 1m

Not physically, no, but I like to think we all live in each other's hearts 👍

Gym

●●●

In today's image-obsessed world, gyms have never been more popular. In my opinion, though, gyms make one critical mistake, leaving a huge opportunity for forward-thinking disruptors like me to exploit.

●●●

8 17:39

Hey. Got your number from sign about free gym membership. This the right number?

Michael *17:58*

Sure is. You interested in a free gym?

 18:00

Yeah, Maybe. Is it an actual gym? How is it free? Give details.

Michael *18:02*

Okay. Imagine, if you will, a typical gym, filled with typical gym equipment.

 18:02

Ok

Michael *18:04*

It's got weights, exercise bikes, treadmills etc.

 18:05

Yes

Michael *18:06*

Now imagine if you could use all
that equipment for free!

 18:07

OK. Sounds good.

Michael *18:13*

Here is a diagram of what it would
look like:

 18:14

Right.

Michael *18:15*

Right. What do you think?

18:16

About what?

Michael *18:17*

About the free gym

 18:20

I still don't know how it works?

Michael *18:22*

I just sent you the diagram of how it works.

 18:23

WTF are you talking about??

Michael *18:29*

That's my concept for a free gym. Obviously there would be more equipment than that but I don't have time to draw all the other stuff right now.

18:33

The sign said free gym
membership.

Michael *18:35*

It IS a free gym. Anyone who wants
to use it can use it for free.

 18:36

I get that but where is the gym?

Michael *18:40*

That hasn't been decided yet. So
far I've only drawn that diagram.
Now we just need to get funding,
find a location, build it and install
the gym equipment

 18:41

F█████s sake

 18:42

Are you for real?

Michael *18:46*

Will contact a builder tomorrow to set the wheels in motion. I'd do it tonight but I've got a meeting with a potential investor about my idea for a free shoe shop.

 18:49

Why does your sign say you're offering free gym membership? Unless i'm missing something, You are clearly not.

Michael *18:51*

I didn't say it was ready immediately. It's still in the concept stage at the moment.

 18:56

That's totally useless. Seriously don't make people think that there's a free gym if there isn't.

Michael *19:00*

If you want to use a gym for free immediately, though, I think there might be a way.

Michael *19:05*

We find someone who has a gym membership and we steal his membership card. Then we'll disguise you to look exactly like him. You could then use his card and go to his gym. I know it's risky but if we do this right, I think it could work.

Michael *19:13*

Hello?

Michael *19:14*

You still there?

Lawnmowing

● ●

There is a reason that lawnmowing is
known as 'the third-oldest profession'.
It is in need of a new approach.

● ●

Michael *14:13*

Hi! Are you interested in hiring the free lawnmower service?

 14:15

Yeah I just walked past this sign and thought might as well send a text. Wouldn't mind a break from it. What's the catch? 😄

Michael *14:19*

There's no catch. A professional gardener will mow your lawn for free. And if you're satisfied with the result, hopefully you'll want to hire me again and recommend me to others.

 14:20

OK Fair enough. Deal.

 14:20

Can I book it now?

Michael *14:22*

Of course. When would you like your lawn to be mowed?

 14:25

Anytime tomorrow (Friday) afternoon? Or Tuesday afternoon if that's too short notice. Address is ███████████████

Michael *14:26*

Tomorrow is fine. Will you be available to help out?

 14:26

Help out how?

Michael *14:28*

Well, the way I do it, it's a 2-person job.

 14:29

How is it 2 person?

Michael *14:31*

Because I don't actually mow lawns myself (I tried to mow my dad's lawn once in 2003 but I didn't really enjoy it so I got him to take over while I went indoors for a nap). Don't worry though because I think I know a way that we can get your lawn mowed for free.

 14:33

Do you want to give me details? What does it involved?

Michael *14:36*

Okay, here's how it'll work:

Michael *14:36*

Step 1: You and I meet at your house tomorrow afternoon. From there, we'll go and find a professional gardener who uses a ride-on lawnmower

Michael *14:37*

Step 2: We wait until he's mowing someone else's lawn (hopefully not too far from your house). We will then yell an insult at him (nothing overly hurtful, let's not be mean, but enough to anger him)

Michael *14:38*

Step 3: You and I will then run away, in the direction of your house. The gardener will be so angry about us insulting him that he will almost certainly start furiously driving after us.

Michael *14:39*

Step 4: We will then lead him to your house, where we will start running up and down your lawn in perfectly straight lines.

Michael *14:40*

Step 5: Hopefully the gardener will have forgotten to switch off the mower mechanism so while he continues to angrily chase us, he will unwittingly be mowing your lawn!

Michael *14:41*

Boom! We just got your lawn mowed for free! Perfect plan!

 14:50

I don't every know what to say to that. So no actual free lawnmowing then? Should probably have guessed that was out of the question.

Michael *14:53*

But I just told you exactly how to get free lawn mowing. Do we have a deal? As I said, the first time is free but if you want me to keep tricking professional gardeners into mowing your lawn, you're going to have to pay me. I'm not running a charity here.

Horseriding Lessons

A lot of people are reluctant to provide professional advice to people about things they've never done. This hesitancy/cowardice is not something that affects me. One of my greatest qualities is that I don't feel any need whatsoever to have experience of a subject before telling people how to do it.

FREE HORSERIDING LESSONS!

Start the new year off the right way by trying something different!

Receive 3 FREE horseriding lessons! If you don't like the lessons, no obligation to continue!

You'll be taught by one of the country's leading horseriding experts!

No risk of injury! Health and safety guaranteed!

Simply text the word "Horse" to the number below to get in touch!

086 807 | 086 807 | 086 807 | 086 807 | 086 807 | 086 807 | 086 807 | 086 807 | 086 807 | 086 807 | 086 807 | 086 807 | 086 807 | 086 807

Thursday 10 January 2019

 15:51

Hey is the horse riding lesson available still?

Michael *15:57*

Yep. You interested?

 15:59

Yeah for 2 people if poss?

Michael *16:00*

No problem. Just name a date and time.

 16:01

Still free if its 2 people?

Michael *16:04*

Still free. Just tell me when you'd like to avail of your free lesson. My schedule is very flexible so pick any time you like.

16:11

Wednesday afternoon if poss?

Michael *16:12*

Perfect. I'll be in touch on Wednesday.

 16:13

Where are u based?

Monday 14 January 2019

 13:08

Hey just checking in about the horse riding lesson. Where are u based?

Wednesday 16 January 2019

Michael *14:00*

Your horseriding lesson will begin now.

 14:01

Hey I didn't hear back from you?

Michael *14:03*

You said Wednesday afternoon.

 14:08

I didn't know where your based.
I text a few times and you never
came back?

Michael *14:10*

That's the great thing about my
lessons! Locations are irrelevant
because I teach horseriding
remotely. Are you ready to learn?!

Michael *14:12*

Lesson 1: To be a good horserider,
always remember to SIT on your
horse. Standing on your horse is
very dangerous.

Michael *14:13*

Lesson 2: When horseriding near a cliff, be careful NOT to tumble off the edge.

Michael *14:16*

Lesson 3: When you are finished horseriding, remember to DISMOUNT. This is probably the most important horseriding lesson of all. If you forget to dismount, you will spend the rest of your life on a horse.

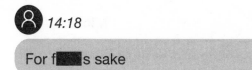

14:18

For f███s sake

Michael *14:19*

Did you enjoy your three free lessons? If so, I can send you more horseriding lessons. Though i should mention that each subsequent lesson costs 12,000 euros

 14:19

No.

Michael *14:21*

Please. I need customers. I quit my job to start this business but, for some reason, it's been disastrously unprofitable. I think maybe there's a flaw in my pricing structure, I'm not sure.

Michael *14:23*

I could also send you lessons on other activities if that's something you'd be interested in? Quad biking? Rock climbing? Scuba diving? Let me know.

Social Media

Social media is increasingly popular nowadays, with some experts estimating that tens of thousands of people now have their own social media account. As such, by becoming a social media expert, you instantly make yourself a potentially valuable and powerful ally. This strategy very nearly earned me my first client AND a new friend.

13:56

Hi. My name is ███████████.
I work with ██████████. Based
at ████████████████. Saw
the ad for social media and just
wondering what's the catch?

Michael *15:29*

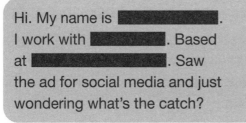

There's no catch. I'm a social media
expert and I enjoy helping companies
to boost their audience for free.

 15:32

So you do this for a living but its
free? How do you get paid?

Michael *15:34*

I'm not in it for the money. Boosting
companies' online presence is my
passion and I would never let that
passion be contaminated by money.

 15:36

That's cool. There aren't many
people like that. Tell me what you
could do for us?

Michael *15:41*

Okay, here is a graph to illustrate the kind of boost in online followers you could expect from availing of my services:

Michael *15:42*

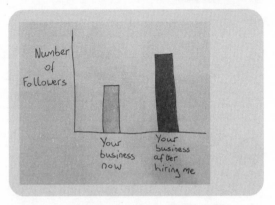

Michael *15:44*

As you can see, the bar on the right is bigger than the bar on the left, thus proving my credentials.

 15:47

Yes but what sort of things do you do to build a target audience? I don't want numbers just for the sake of it. That's pointless. They should be actual customers or potential customers.

Michael *15:52*

I'm glad you asked. I have created
an advanced filtering system which
ensures that my clients get only the
finest followers. Here is a diagram
of how it works:

Michael *15:52*

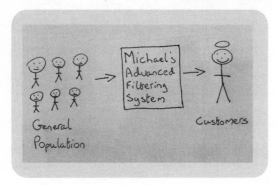

15:55

Right, some detail here work be
good

15:55

would be good

Michael *15:57*

Well, the little circle above the customer's head is a halo. I used that to illustrate that he is a good person and a good customer.

 16:01

No, details on the filtering system. Tell me how it works and tell me how working with you would be in my interest.

Michael *16:11*

Okay, here is a visual overview of the benefits of working with me:

16:14

Ffs. Should have known it was too good to be true. Waste of time. No way are you an expert on social media or anything else.

Michael *16:16*

Are you refusing to hire me just because I like to wear jean shorts to work? Because that's discrimination.

Michael *16:19*

I no longer wish to be considered for the position of your company's social media consultant. I do NOT work for businesses that are prejudiced against people in jean shorts.

Guitar Lessons

Do not be afraid to be forthright about business etiquette, as friendship can only ever come from a place of absolute honesty. If you are a coward, you'll keep your mouth shut and let it slide, thus resulting in a toxic friendship that will never grow into something special. If you are like me, though, you'll call them out on their behaviour. My experience is that your friendship will ultimately be stronger for it. I'm almost entirely sure of that.

Chris  · 2 hrs

Hey all, hope its cool for me to post this here. I'm offering guitar lessons remotely. (Zoom, Skype etc) If anyone wants to get guitar lessons themself or buy for someone you think will enjoy them hit me up in the DMs or call me on

Have long list of references so you'll be getting someone who knows what they are doing. Obvs you'll need access to your own guitar! £10 for the first lesson with no obligation.

Thanks!

6 likes   13 comments

 **Michael** · 51m

Suspect it's not a coincidence that you've chosen to charge exactly £10 for the first lesson. Bit sneaky but I guess all's fair in business

 **Chris** ▬▬▬ · 39m

Michael What do you mean?

 **Michael** · 35m

Feels like a not very subtle attempt to undercut my uncle, who's one of the most renowned guitar instructors in town

 **Bob** ▬▬▬▬ · 32m

Michael Who's your uncle?

 **Michael** · 29m

My dad's brother. Don't have any uncles on my mother's side

Bob  • 24m

His name, Michael. If he's so renowned, tell us his name?

Chris • 22m

Just so you know I've never tried to under cut anyone. I've been offering first lessons for £10 since started in 2016. Nothing to do with under cutting anyone just the price people are willing to pay and still makes it worth my while.

Ⓜ **Michael** • 18m

I'm not saying you're doing anything illegal. Would just question the ethics of it 👍

Bob  • 13m

There's nothing unethical about Chris charging a tenner for a first lesson. Plenty of instructors will have a policy of giving a £10 trial. I'm sure he's not going to give away all future lessons for that.

 **Chris** ▮▮▮▮▮▮ · 11m

Exactly Bob.

Ⓜ **Michael** · 8m

Yes but setting it at exactly £10 feels like a targeted attack on my uncle's pricing policy

 **Bob** ▮▮▮▮▮▮▮ · 5m

How much does he charge?

Ⓜ **Michael** · 2m

£10.01

Michael The Magician

People often ask me, 'Michael, what is the most magical thing in the world?' And to me, the answer is simple: the time David Copperfield made the Statue of Liberty disappear. I mean, how can a huge statue like that just disappear? It doesn't make sense. But the second most magical thing in the world is friendship. So it only makes sense to use magic as a means of establishing new friendships.

For Hire: Free Magician

Hi. I am Michael and I am available to hire as a magician. If you need a magician for an event (birthday party, wedding reception, funeral etc.) I would make a good choice. As well as being good at magic, I am free. This is because I believe it is wrong to charge for a precious artform like magic. To make a booking, simply text "magic" to the number below.

Michael

086 807 086 807 086 808 086 807 086 807 086 807 086 807 086 807 086 808 086 808 086 807 086 807 086 807 086 807

16:36

Magic

Michael *16:56*

Hi! Thank you for your interest in booking Michael The Magician. This is an automated service. For which of the following events do you wish to book Michael The Magician?

A. Birthday Party
B. Wedding Reception
C. Funeral
D. Other - please state

 16:58

A. Birthday party

Michael *17:01*

You have selected Birthday Party. Will there be children at this birthday party?
A. Yes
B. No
C. Yes but Michael The Magician can still do the adult-themed parts of his show, we'll just cover the children's eyes

17:02

A

Michael *17:03*

To confirm you are within travelling distance, please write the address at which you would like Michael The Magician to perform.

17:05

46

Michael *17:07*

If anything goes wrong with Michael The Magician's performance, do you promise not to sue him and/or yell at him?

A. Yes
B. No
C. Not sure

17:08

C

Michael *17:12*

Thank you for selecting Yes. Please state the date on which you would like Michael The Magician to perform (dd/mm/yyyy).

 17:19

10/08/2018

Michael *17:21*

Michael The Magician is unavailable on this date as he will be attending a court case regarding an unfortunate mishap at a show he performed in January. He offers full assurance that he has since successfully mastered the 'Sawing a volunteer in half' trick. Please select another date (dd/mm/yyyy).

 17:22

11/08/2018

Michael *17:24*

You have booked Michael The Magician for 11/08/2018 at 46 ███████████. The total cost of the performance is €840 or an equal value in large hams. Payment can be made on the day.

 17:28

Cancel booking. The sign said its free

Michael *17:30*

Thank you for confirming your booking of Michael The Magician. If you would like to provide feedback on this automated service, please do so now with your rating out of 10.

 17:33

Cancel booking. Sign said free magician. Notice word free. Not interested in paying for this. Am out.

Michael *17:34*

The rating out of 10 that you have selected is not valid. Please try again. Remember to only use numbers.

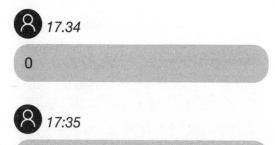 17.34

0

17:35

Scam

Michael *17:36*

Would you like to continue receiving information about Michael The Magician?

A. Subscribe me from this service
B. Unsubscribe me to this service

 17:37

B

Michael *17:38*

Thank you for subscribing.
As a subscriber, you will receive information about upcoming shows, quiz questions and interesting trivia about Michael The Magician.

Michael *17:41*

TRIVIA: Michael The Magician used to be known only as 'Michael'. But that all changed when he received a magic set as a gift on his 26th birthday. On that day his magical journey began.

 17:44

Blocking this number. Don't show up ay my house. Don't say something is free when its not

 17:45

False advertising scam

Michael *17:48*

QUIZ QUESTION: Michael The Magician famously once made a horse disappear. But can you remember the name of the horse?

The Myth
of Failure

You miss 100 per cent of the shots you don't take.
So if you take 150 per cent of the shots, you might hit
100 per cent of them. That's basic mathematics.

A lot of people think that just because I'm a
successful businessman who is popular with ladies
and has countless prospective friends, 100 per
cent of my ideas must work out perfectly. Not true.
Sometimes I'll think of an idea that's so far ahead of
its time people aren't ready to team up with me yet.
What follows are some posters I stuck up around
town that resulted in a shocking lack of response.

Boy Band

Wanted: Boy Band Members

Hi. I am Michael and I am forming a boy band. If you want to join, be here at 10.43am on Monday for auditions. After a rigorous selection process during which I will evaluate your skills as a singer, dancer and heart-throb, I will then choose the best 3 applicants to join the band. We will be called The Friendship Boys and, as well as being in a band together, we will also be best friends who hang out together all the time. I will be the lead singer of the band and we will do songs about fun subjects like dancing and love and snuggling but we will also do songs about hard-hitting topics like economics and the futility of war.

All band members will be expected to contribute to the cost of the tour bus that I have hired (it is surprisingly expensive). Also, you will need to have a passport in case we are asked to do a world tour. Please don't be late on Monday because we have our first gig later that day.

Michael

Live Concert

The Friendship Boys

- Debut performance
- Here on Monday at 2.37pm
- Featuring songs from their upcoming album, including:
  - "Dancing with a Lady"
  - "In Love with a Lady"
  - "Trickle-Down Economics and its Disastrous Social Consequences"
  - "Snuggle Time with a Lady"
  - "The Brutal Savagery of the 1870 Franco-Prussian War"

PLEASE ENSURE THAT YOU ONLY BUY OFFICIALLY-LICENSED FRIENDSHIP BOYS MERCHANDISE. ANYONE CAUGHT SELLING BOOTLEG FRIENDSHIP BOYS MERCHANDISE WILL BE PROSECUTED.

Funeral DJ

For Hire: Funeral DJ

Hi. I am Michael and I am starting a new career as a funeral DJ. If you need someone to play a sad set at a funeral, check out my mixtape below. It features a mournful ballad that I composed and sung myself, a heart-wrenching mash-up of MMMBop and My Heart Will Go On, as well as me performing a beautiful rap about the afterlife. In addition, I also make these promises to all my clients:

- **Punctuality:** I will try to be on time for the funeral
- **Respect:** My set will tastefully cater to the wishes of the bereaved. If you don't want me to play my controversial song, "He's Dead and Someone Here Killed Him," I will not play it
- **Magic:** As well as being a funeral DJ, I'm also an amateur magician. Does this mean I can use magic to reanimate your loved one? No because that would be unethical. But I could still do some basic magic tricks if you want?
- **Post-Funeral Friendship:** Upon losing a loved one, many people feel a void in their life. That is where I come in by becoming your new best friend. We can go to the cinema, hang out at the beach, get matching tattoos etc. I have a lot of free time so I'll be available to hang out a lot

If you like my mixtape, get in touch. Once you've listened to the tape, please reattach it to the poster so that other potential clients can listen it too. It is my only tape so be careful with it. Also, I should mention that I do not own DJ decks but don't worry because I will borrow some from a friend.

Michael

Wanted: DJ Decks

Hi. I am Michael and I need to borrow some DJ decks for several upcoming funerals at which I am performing.

Karate Lawyer

For Hire: Karate Lawyer

Hi. I am Michael and I am pleased to announce that I have launched this town's first karate-based law firm. While many lawyers win cases with knowledge of the law and clever legal arguments, I intend to win mine with karate. Here are some of the services I provide:

- Taking out corrupt judges with karate
- Using karate to defeat prosecution lawyers who are making convincing arguments as to why my client should be imprisoned
- Removing unhelpful jury members with karate
- Using karate to get immunity for my clients (not sure how this will work yet but I will figure it out at the trial)

If you are being persecuted by the law and need a lawyer, take one of my business cards below and get in touch. What I lack in formal legal qualifications, I make up for in karate moves.

Michael

Michael
The Karate Lawyer

If you are tired of hiring lawyers who know the law but DON'T know karate, hire The Karate Lawyer. It's like hiring a real lawyer but better because he does karate.

@Michael1979

Karate Lawyer – Clarification

Hi. Michael again from the poster above. Following a heated discussion with a policeman, I have been asked to make it clear that I am not legally allowed to represent defendants in a court of law and, even if I was, I would not be allowed to do karate on anyone. As a result, my karate law firm is closed for the foreseeable future. I will, however be starting a new business very soon.

Michael

For Hire: Karate Architect

Hi. I am Michael and I am pleased to announce that I have become this town's first karate-based architect.

Computer Hacker

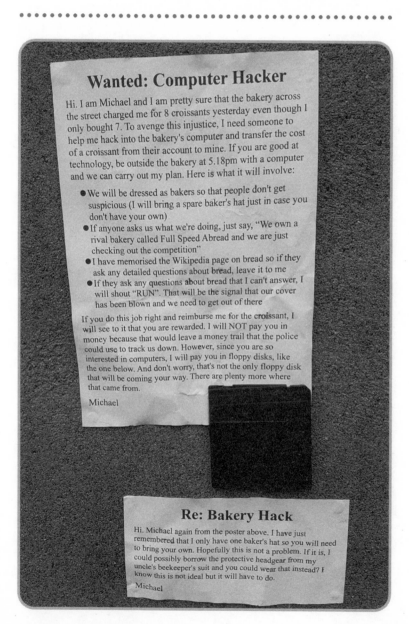

Wanted: Computer Hacker

Hi. I am Michael and I am pretty sure that the bakery across the street charged me for 8 croissants yesterday even though I only bought 7. To avenge this injustice, I need someone to help me hack into the bakery's computer and transfer the cost of a croissant from their account to mine. If you are good at technology, be outside the bakery at 5.18pm with a computer and we can carry out my plan. Here is what it will involve:

- We will be dressed as bakers so that people don't get suspicious (I will bring a spare baker's hat just in case you don't have your own)
- If anyone asks us what we're doing, just say, "We own a rival bakery called Full Speed Abread and we are just checking out the competition"
- I have memorised the Wikipedia page on bread so if they ask any detailed questions about bread, leave it to me
- If they ask any questions about bread that I can't answer, I will shout "RUN". That will be the signal that our cover has been blown and we need to get out of there

If you do this job right and reimburse me for the croissant, I will see to it that you are rewarded. I will NOT pay you in money because that would leave a money trail that the police could use to track us down. However, since you are so interested in computers, I will pay you in floppy disks, like the one below. And don't worry, that's not the only floppy disk that will be coming your way. There are plenty more where that came from.

Michael

Re: Bakery Hack

Hi. Michael again from the poster above. I have just remembered that I only have one baker's hat so you will need to bring your own. Hopefully this is not a problem. If it is, I could possibly borrow the protective headgear from my uncle's beekeeper's suit and you could wear that instead? I know this is not ideal but it will have to do.

Michael

Haircut

Wanted: Haircut

Hi. I am Michael and I need a haircut. My usual hairdresser is on holiday so I am hiring someone else to do it. If you are free tomorrow and are a professional hairdresser, this is your opportunity to get to cut my hair. Here is the information you will need to know:

- Be here tomorrow at 10.27am with all your hairdressing equipment
- I will walk by at that time. It will be easy for you to recognise me because I will be the person whose hair is slightly too long
- When you see me, you will walk over to me and start cutting my hair
- I prefer to have my hair cut in complete silence so please do NOT attempt to engage me in conversation
- I sometimes have second thoughts about getting haircuts so there is a chance that I may resist and try to fight you off. Please rest assured, though, that this is just nerves and I really do want you to cut my hair. So, no matter how much I struggle, know that I need this haircut and I give you permission to pin me down for as long as necessary so that you can administer my haircut

Once the haircut is complete, I will say, "Thank you, kindly hairdresser." If you do not hear those exact words, that was not me and I probably got delayed or something. I will definitely be along sometime before lunch, though.

Michael

Piano Lessons

Wanted: Piano Lesson

Hi. I am Michael and I need to learn how to play the piano before Saturday. My parents have been paying for me to get piano lessons every week for the last thirty years but I never actually attended any of the lessons and I spent the money on candles instead. Now they want me to play Beethoven's 5th Symphony at their wedding anniversary on Saturday.

If you can teach me, be here tomorrow at 11.06am with a grand piano. I am a fast learner (I once memorised the lyrics to "MMMBop" by Hanson in less than eight hours) so I am pretty sure I will pick it up quickly. In return, I can teach you some cool wrestling moves or tell you some facts about helicopters. Whichever you prefer. Not both, though.

Michael

For sale: Candles (1986 – present)

Hi. I am Michael and I am selling my candle collection. If you are interested, be here on Friday at 9.11am so that we open negotiations. I will accept cash or, preferably, trades for other candles.

Ghost Hunter

For Hire: Ghost Hunter

Hi. I am Michael and I am the foremost ghost hunter in this part of town. I investigate any kind of paranormal activity and report back with my findings. It is like The X-Files but without the drawback of having to explain my conclusions to a scientist. Here are some of my skills:

- Good at sensing the presence of ghosts
- Have my own ouija board (I am almost certain I once contacted John Lennon via this method)
- Climbing
- Bravery... but also caution
- In 2011, I solved The Mystery of the Haunted Bus (if you don't know about it, look it up)

If you want to avail of my services, please take one of my business cards below and get in touch. I know it says "goat hunter" but that is a misprint. The lady in the shop misheard me when I said "ghost hunter" and I can't afford to get all 250,000 cards reprinted.

Michael

Michael
Goat Hunter

For all your goat-hunting needs

Hunting goats since 2004. Or maybe 2005, I'm not sure. Can't remember. Definitely no later than 2006, though.

Michael

The best goat-hunter in this part of town.

Wedding Partner

Wanted: Wedding Partner

Hi. I am Michael and I need a partner for my sister's wedding on Friday. If you are interested, I will pick you up here on Friday at 12.56am. All you need to do is pretend to be in a relationship with me and answer any questions my relatives ask about us. Here is a history of our relationship that you will need to memorise:

- We met in a karate dojo last January
- We are both good at karate (yellow belt)
- Our favourite film is The Karate Kid (you will need to watch this before Friday in case anyone questions you on it)
- My favourite thing about you is your smile
- Your favourite thing about me is my leg sweep
- Our favourite historical figure is Bruce Lee
- You come from a long line of karate enthusiasts, most notably your maternal great grandfather who managed a dojo between the 1st and 2nd world wars
- We have done k*ssing (once after a karate bout and once before a karate seminar)

In return, you will get a free meal. It is not a free bar but my cousin Martin will have cans of beer in his car and I will get you one (two at most). This is a one-time deal. I am not interested in a relationship at the moment because I am focusing on my karate career.

Michael

Holidays

Being a professional business person is not easy. The stresses and strains of businessing pile up. Never be afraid to admit you need a break from it all and enjoy a lovely holiday with a close friend.

WIN A HOLIDAY!

Need a break from it all?

Want a 2-week getaway with someone special to a destination of your choice?

To be in with a chance of winning a dream holiday, simply text "HOLIDAY" to the number below.

086 807 086 807 086 807 086 807 086 807 086 807 086 807 086 807 086 807   086 807 086 807 086 807 086 807

 14:24

Holiday

Michael *14:27*

Hi, who's this?

 14:31

Sean ████████. Was texting about a holiday competition. Sorry if wrong number

Michael *14:32*

You have the right number. The winner will be chosen shortly!

Michael *16:50*

Congratulations, Sean! You have been selected as the winner!

 16:51

Serious???

Michael *16:55*

Can you be at Dublin airport at 7:12am tomorrow?

 16:58

Tomorrow? Not sure. Probably not. Have work tomorrow.

Michael *17:03*

No, it's all arranged for tomorrow.

 17:04

Any where in the world? This for 2 weeks for 2 people yes?

Michael *17:05*

Yeah, just the two of us.

 17:07

Us? Who is us?

Michael *17:07*

You and me.

 17:08

Who are you?

Michael *17:09*

I'm Michael

17:11

So it's a holiday with some random guy I don't know 😂

Michael *17:13*

I know we don't know one another very well right now but we can get to know each other while we're on holiday and become friends.

 17:16

😂 Thanks but no thanks. If this is real someone else can have it

Michael *17:17*

You don't want your free holiday?

 17:20

Hows it free? Are you seriously offering to paying for me to go on holiday?

Michael *17:22*

No need. I've figured out a way that we can get free flights to anywhere in the world.

17:24

How?

Michael *17:25*

Okay, here's how it'll work:

Michael *17:28*

We'll meet at the airport at 7:12am tomorrow. We'll then go directly to the pilots' lounge and find a pilot and co-pilot who are scheduled to fly the same flight.

Michael *17:30*

We'll then challenge them to a game of strip poker. Hopefully we'll win and then, when they're undressed, we'll steal their uniforms and put them on.

Michael *17:32*

Then, disguised as pilots, we'll be able to go through the pilots' entrance to the plane. If anyone asks any technical questions, just let me do the talking. I have memorised the first seven paragraphs of the wikipedia page on Aviation so that should cover almost everything.

Michael *17:34*

Once we're in the cockpit, we'll have a few minutes to figure out how everything works. That should be more than enough.

Michael *17:35*

We'll then fly to wherever you want to go on holiday. Nowhere too hot, though, because my skin peels in the sun.

Michael *17:36*

I know this plan is heavily dependent on us winning the strip poker game but don't worry. I'm going to learn how to play tonight and hopefully I'll be good at it. Also, I'm not sure yet how we're going to get home but we can figure that out later.

 17:40

Can't believe I thought this was serious 😂 😂 😂

Michael *17:46*

Are you sure I can't change your mind? Here's a computer-generated image I've mocked up to show how much fun we'd have on holiday:

Michael *17:47*

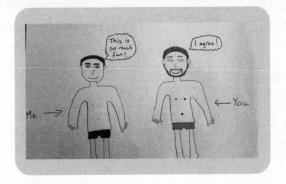

Part II

Pleasure

Making Friends

As we have seen, there can be a tragic downside to trying to make friends in business, which is that people don't always appreciate your ingenious business ideas and sometimes get angry at you for being ahead of your time. You mustn't ever let that affect you, though. Friendship is too important to take onboard things that people say to you.

So when that fails, you need to think big. And there's nothing bigger than the information superhighway. By getting yourself online, you can find an unlimited number of group chats and Facebook groups to join and that's where you'll find the most friends. Incidentally, don't worry about whether or not anyone actually wants you in the group. Most people don't know what they want and you can't let minor details like that get in the way.

What follows are strategies for finding, nurturing, keeping and expanding friendships.

Group Admin Group Chat

There are two types of people in the world: followers and leaders. I am very much one of the latter and I've found that sometimes you've got to seize control in order to implement your ideas and prove to others that you are their superior in the group chat. There will often be a few objections from defeated opponents but at the end of it, you will almost certainly have earned everybody's respect and the group chat will be a better place. And even if you haven't earned everyone's respect and the group chat isn't a better place, I find it's much easier to silence dissent from a position of impregnable power.

Group and Sandwiches

28 August 2019

Paul: 12:25

Signing out for the next week, lads. Off to Tunisia and having a digital detox. Behave yourselves while I'm gone 👋

Michael: 12:26

Can I be group admin until you come back?

<You're now an admin>

Michael: 12:28

Thank you for this great honour. Being made a Group Administrator is the highest honour a citizen can receive and I will not let you down.

30 August 2019

Michael: 21:02

Hi all. Now that I'm the group admin, I think it's time to discuss some serious matters. I've been monitoring the quality of the posts in this group and I'm worried that standards are slipping. I've decided that I will start randomly selecting posts and give them a rating out of 9. If that post earns less than a 5/9 rating, the sender will be ejected from the group. This is the only way to ensure people are submitting the highest quality posts.

Phil: 21:40

Lee: 21:44

Looking forward to all my posts getting 9/9

31 August 2019

Bill: 11:31

What's the 3pm TV game today anyone know?

Michael: 11:33

👆 The above post, submitted by Bill, gets a 2/9 rating. Thank you for your contributions to the group, Bill, but your post has fallen below the standards expected of this group. We wish you well and hope you find success in other group chats.

<You removed Bill>

Alan: 11:38

You actually removed him
I'm dead 😄

Michael: 11:51

👆 The above post, submitted by Alan, gets a 4/9 rating. Thank you for your contributions to the group, Alan, but your post has fallen below the standards expected of this group. We wish you well and hope you find success in other group chats.

\<You removed Alan\>

Michael: 11:54

Right, now that we've got rid of the people who were holding us back with substandard posts, I really feel like this group is back on track. Looking forward to seeing some great posts!

Michael: 11:55

👆 The above post, submitted by Michael, gets a 9/9 rating. Just an excellent, excellent post.

Ed: 12:16

Very good. Can i re-add them now or are we teaching them a lesson for a few hours?

Michael: 12:40

👆 The above post, submitted by Ed, gets a 1/9 rating. Thank you for your contributions to the group, Ed, but your post has fallen below the standards expected of this group. We wish you well and hope you find success in other group chats.

<You removed Ed>

Michael: 19:21

I notice that some of you are remaining silent out of fear that I will rate your post unfavourably. Your cowardice MUST be punished. Cowards get an automatic 0/9

<You removed Phil>

<You removed Marco>

<You removed Lee>

Today

Paul: 12:32

I see that making you admin worked out well then. Ffs

Michael: 12:33

I was just trying to improve the standard of posts :(

Parking Ticket

Always remember that people appreciate a friend who can give advice and offer a new angle on a problem they're struggling with.

 David ▪▪▪▪▪▪▪▪▪▪ • 9 hrs

Literally can't believe parking restrictions still being enforced around town. Just got a ticket for parking on the road outside Tesco (had no choice because car park was full). Jobsworth traffic warden giving people tickets in middle of pandemic. Pathetic and disgusting.

2 likes   41 comments

 **Michael** · 7h

Hi David. My uncle got a ticket for parking on that same road on Friday but he managed to get it written off this morning 👍

David ▮▮▮▮▮▮ · 6h

Michael What did he do?

 **Michael** · 6h

He parked illegally on the road outside Tesco

David ▮▮▮▮▮▮ · 6h

I know that but what did he do to get the ticket written off?

 **Michael** · 6h

Well, he's got an ingenious little trick that he uses to get out of paying parking tickets. Bit sneaky but it always works 👍

David ▮▮▮▮▮▮▮ · 6h

What does he do?

Michael · 6h

He's the assistant manager in a hardware shop

David ▮▮▮▮▮▮▮ · 6h

?

David ▮▮▮▮▮▮▮ · 6h

Are you taking the piss?

Michael · 6h

No. Why?

David ▮▮▮▮▮▮▮ · 6h

Because I obviously meant what does he do to get out of paying parking tickets? That's what the post is about. Why would I want to know what your uncle does for a living?

 **Michael** · 6h

Oh, okay. Sorry. I thought you were just curious.

David ▮▮▮▮▮ · 6h

I'm curious abuot how he gets out of paying parking tickets? What's the trick?

 **Michael** · 6h

Okay, so, as I mentioned, he has a little trick that he uses and it always works. He learned it from a friend of his who he met while working as a translator in Norway.

David ▮▮▮▮▮ · 6h

What is it?

 **Michael** · 6h

It's a country in Scandinavia right beside Sweden.

David ▮▮▮▮▮ · 6h

 F▮▮ing idiot

Burglary Group Chat

Don't be afraid to share your problems with your friends too. We all go through tough times and a problem shared is a problem halved. Or, if there's lots of people in the residents' group chat you've managed to get yourself added to, a problem shared is a problem divided by, like, 28.

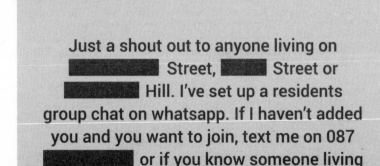

Rachel ▮▮▮▮▮▮ • 22 hrs

Just a shout out to anyone living on ▮▮▮▮▮▮▮ Street, ▮▮▮▮ Street or ▮▮▮▮▮▮▮ Hill. I've set up a residents group chat on whatsapp. If I haven't added you and you want to join, text me on 087 ▮▮▮▮▮▮▮ or if you know someone living in the area and think they should be in, feel free to let them know. Thanks! 🙏 🩶

19 likes   16 comments 2 shares

Residents

Michael: 17:12

Hey, did any of you see anything suspicious this morning? Someone robbed my house so am looking for clues

Chloe: 17:13

Oh God, so sorry to hear Michael. Is everyone OK?

Sean: 17:16

Didn't see anything. Whic house is yours?

Rachel: 17:18

So sorry 2 hear this. What street are you on Michael? Hope ur ok. Are you living alone? 🩶

Cillian: 17:18

Do you have CCTV?

Michael: 17:20

Yeah, I have 12 security cameras but nobody showed up on any of them

Sean: 17:21

Have you reported it?

Michael: 17:21

Yeah, the police are refusing to help, though, so I'm doing my own investigation

Sean: 17:22

Ok let us know if there's anything we can do.

Michael: 17:23

Just looking for alibis for each of you for this morning if that's okay. Am not accusing anyone, just want to eliminate you all from my inquiries. Thanks.

Sean: 17:25

I've been at work all day but I don't think you need to worry about alibis. Everyone I know here is really decent.

Michael: 17:26

What's the number of your place of work? Just want to give them a quick call to confirm your whereabouts

Chloe: 17:29

I know it's stressful but I wouldn't go down the road of accusing people. What street do you live on? If you need help cleaning up or anything just say the world and we'll be round with the brooms! 🩶

Michael: 17:30

No, they didn't make a mess. They just took the TV remote control

Chloe: 17:31

Okay

Siobhan: 17:31

??????

Siobhan: 17:32

No mess and they only took a
remote control??

Michael: 17:33

Yeah, I guess maybe someone
disturbed them so they must have
only had time to grab the remote

Siobhan: 17:34

Sorry but nobody breaks in ti a
house and only steals a remote
control

Sean: 17:36

Also, they weren't seen on any of
the 12 security cameras 🤔

Siobhan: 17:37

They took the remote but left the TV???

Michael: 17:38

Don't know if you're being deliberately obtuse but remote controls are easier to carry than TVs so it makes sense

Siobhan: 17:39

I'm not being obtuse it's just a remote control is no use without a telly

Michael: 17:40

I know but they might have been planning to buy the same TV and now they can get a discount because they won't have to buy the remote control for it

Cillian: 17:40

Michael. Was there forced entry? Broken Window/ door?

Michael: 17:41

No, am thinking they must have used the chimney

Sean: 17:43

Excuse my language but for f████ 's sake. You had the whole neighbourhood panicked about a burglary because you lost a remote control?

Michael: 17:45

Sorry, hadn't realised it only qualifies as a burglary if a Ming vase and a couple of Picassos get stolen. You 1%ers are so out of touch

Sean: 17:46

I didn't say that, did I? Just don't think anyone stole your poxy remote control.

Sean: 17:47

What house you live at btw? I notice you didn't answer when I asked earlier.

Michael: 17:48

And I notice you didn't answer when I asked for everybody to provide alibis for their whereabouts this morning. Interesting…

Sean: 17:49

I told you I was at work you nutter. Have you even looked for for your remote control or you just prefer accusing people?

Michael: 17:52

Okay, quick update on my investigation. Turns out they didn't 'steal' the remote control as such. They just hid it between the cushions of my sofa. Which is even worse when you think about it. Why would someone want to mess with me like that? There are some real sickos out there, imo

<Chloe removed you>

You can't send messages to this group because you're no longer a participant.

Songwriting Partner

Wanted: Songwriting Partner

Hi. I am Michael and I want to form a songwriting duo. If you are interested, meet me here tomorrow at 10.39am. I have already written the lyrics for twelve songs that will form the basis of our first album. Three of them are about dolphins (2 electro-punk, 1 rap). One of them is about the deceased wrestler Andre The Giant (ballad). Eight of them are about Hitler's decision to attack Russia in 1941 (all disco). We just need to put them to music.

I expect the whole process to take us three hours. If you have any instruments, bring them with you. I will ask my cousin Martin if we can borrow his ukulele. If he says no, I will do beatboxing instead.

Michael

Mystery Speedos

Sometimes a useful friendship strategy can be dropping a metaphorical bomb in a group chat and then ignoring all questions. This is a very effective way of finding out who cracks under pressure.

"2018/19 Season"

Stephen: 14:03

Lose tomorrow and I reckon he's gone

Fionn: 14:04

Yeh think ur prob right

Michael: 14:05

Hey guys. I know I only joined the group yesterday and I don't want to embarrass anyone but a member of this group took it upon himself this morning to private message me raunchy photos of himself proudly lounging in some very snug speedos. There's no judgement here and I'm not offended but I was looking to join a group that focuses exclusively on football. I wasn't looking for anything extra. Thanks for inviting me, though. It was great to meet you all.

Fionn: 14:06

the f██k??

Niall: 14:06

Who did that?

Darragh: 14:08

Very snug speedo's   def not me I couldn't fit in speedos these days

Conor: 14:08

This is amazing!!

Matt: 14:09

We do focus on football

Niall: 14:09

Name names! Who thr f█k is sending speedo pics???

Conor: 14:10

Whose even wearing speedos in 2019

Josh: 14:10

Is this for real?

Conor: 14:12

Proudly lounging in very snug speedos is an incredible sentence

Edwin: 14:13

I need to know who this was

JB: 14:13

Not me

Ciaran: 14:14

Not me

Thomas: 14:14

PM me the name Michael

Jordan: 14:15

Wasn't me

Niall: 14:15

Please name names I beg you

<You left>

You can't send messages to this group because you're no longer a participant.

New Aldi

You must always remember that where friendship is concerned, it is very much the thought that counts. Would it help if you had even the slightest knowledge of the topic in question? Yes. But is it essential? Absolutely not.

 Jane ▮▮▮▮▮▮▮▮ • 3 hrs

Anyone have any info on if the new Aldi opening is going ahead? Thinking it's could be delayed because of corona virus? Would be handy x

11 likes   27 comments

 **Alan** ▬▬▬ • 2h

Supposed to open in September from what I heard.

 **Jane** ▬▬▬▬ • 2h

I heard that too but wondering if it will be delayed what with everything going on

 **John** ▬▬▬ • 2h

Can't see it opening in Sep now. Expect a delay till 2021 I'd say.

Ⓜ **Michael** • 2h

My uncle was hired to be the assistant site manager on that project so he's been able to tell me all the latest information 👍

 **Alan** ▬▬▬ • 2h

Michael Which is?

 **Michael** • 2h

It just basically means he's second in command and whenever the manager is off site, my uncle becomes the person in charge

 **Alan** ▮▮▮▮▮▮▮ • 2h

Mate I get that, I was talking about what's the latest information?

 **Michael** • 2h

Haven't spoken to him for a couple of days. I'll give him a call now and see what he says.

 **Jane** ▮▮▮▮▮▮▮▮ • 1h

Thanks **Michael** 🍻

 **Michael** • 36m

Sorry for the delay but just spoke to my uncle if anyone's interested in hearing the latest information?

John ▮▮▮▮▮▮ • 33m

Yup!

Jane ▮▮▮▮▮▮▮▮ • 28m

Michael Yes what did he say?

Ⓜ **Michael** • 12m

Thought you'd ask that and I didn't want you to miss anything so I wrote out the minutes of our conversation:

Ⓜ **Michael** • 8m

- We opened with greetings. I said 'Hi, how are you?', Uncle Geoffrey said, 'Afternoon, Michael, good to speak to you.'

- I asked him how he is. Uncle Geoffrey replied, 'Not too bad but my neck has been playing up a bit.' I said, 'I'm sorry to hear that.' He said, 'Thanks.'

- The conversation then moved on to gardening. Uncle Geoffrey said he had been doing a lot of work on his garden and he said his lawn is looking better than it has in years. I asked him to send me a picture of it. He said he would.

- We then discussed Nan. Apparently her arthritis has been giving her a few problems so she's going to speak to her doctor about the possibility of trying a different medication. We both agreed that this was a sensible approach.

- Uncle Geoffrey asked me if I had heard from my cousin Martin recently. I said I had.

- I then mentioned to Uncle Geoffrey that I'm in a Facebook group with people who want to know about the new Aldi supermarket for which he's the assistant site manager. Uncle Geoffrey then informed me that I was mistaken and that he has no involvement in the new Aldi supermarket. I apologised. He told me not to worry about it.

- We then said our goodbyes and agreed to speak again over the weekend.

2 likes

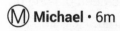 **Michael** · 6m

Hopefully that clears things up for you guys. Been nice talking to you all 👍

Amazing Pics (PG)

The good thing about finding friends who share your passions is that you have an intense connection, but the bad thing is that they can get a little rambunctious. That's why you'll sometimes need to step in and cool things down before they get too s*xy.

19 February 2020

William: 12:13

Nelson's Pillar in Dublin after the bombing in 1966

Hannah: 12:14

Wow had never seen this before. Thanks for posting.

William: 12:15

Really interesting story behind it too.

Michael: 12:17

Just want to remind you all that pics in this group are supposed to be PG. No adult material. Please delete the above pic and keep it clean from now on or you'll be removed.

Hannah: 12:18

Huh?

John: 12:18

What's wrong with it?

Michael: 12:19

Very ph*llic image. Not appropriate.

William: 12:20

Get the f█k out of here with that snowflake bullshit. It's a historical photo. Grow up.

Michael: 12:24

I know but sometimes history can be inappropriately s*xy.

26 February 2020

Phillipa: 10:04

Spiral galaxy. 175000 light years across.

Michael: 10:09

PG images ONLY. Please delete the above pic or you'll be removed. Thanks.

Phillipa: 10:10

My pic?

Michael: 10:16

Yes, your pic. That 'spiral galaxy' pic is obscene.

Phillipa: 10:22

I don't understand. How is that obscene?

Michael: 10:24

Looks like a bre*st with a n*pple at the centre.

William: 10:25

Ignore him, Phil. He tried to pull me up on a pic of Nelson's pillar last week. Snowflake bullshit. Offended by everything.

Benjy: 10:25

Guarantee you only one person saw a breast in that pic and its you Michael.

Michael: 10:28

Thank you. I have a good eye for spotting inappropriate content 👍

William: 10:35

It wasn't inappropriate you sanctimonious dickhead. No one else had a problem with it.

Michael: 10:41

That doesn't make it right

Today

BDD: 16:03

View of the night sky from the
Atacama Desert

Michael: 16:15

Please delete. No salacious images.
PG posts ONLY.

Benjy: 16:22

What is your problem? You get
offended by half the posts in here
not being PG and there's nothing
wrong with them,

BDD: 16:25

What's wrong with it

Michael: 16:35

Too racy. If you draw lines between some of the brightest stars (excluding the two middles ones), it looks like a br*

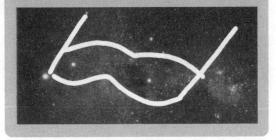

Michael: 16:35

Totally inappropriate.

William: 16:46

Bra is not a rude word you f⬛⬛ing weirdo

Michael: 16:59

We'll have to agree to disagree on that but in the meantime, I'm imposing a ban on astronomy pics that look like br*s

Benjy: 17:03

Can't even be dealing with you anymore.

<Benjy removed you>

You can't send messages to this group because you're no longer a participant.

ISS

· ·

It's important to be selective in who you
befriend. I, for example, have a non-negotiable policy
of never befriending terrorists. Sadly, some people
online are not so careful. I would advise anyone
reading this who thinks they have potentially been
radicalised to turn themselves in immediately
by emailing enquiries.FBI@hotmail.com.

· ·

Glen  · 5 hrs

Some sighting opportunities of the ISS over the next few nights for anyone interested

Fri Mar 27, 7:41 PM	5 min	63°	22° above WSW	11° above E
Fri Mar 27, 9:16 PM	3 min	42°	10° above W	42° above SW
Sat Mar 28, 8:30 PM	3 min	57°	18° above W	36° above SE
Sat Mar 28, 11:06 PM	< 1 min	13°	11° above W	13° above W
Sun Mar 29, 8:43 PM	4 min	62°	32° above WSW	11° above ESE
Sun Mar 29, 10:18 PM	2 min	27°	11° above W	27° above SW
Mon Mar 30, 9:32 PM	3 min	39°	17° above W	28° above SSE
Tue Mar 31, 8:45 PM	4 min	48°	30° above WSW	11° above ESE

8 likes   19 comments

 **Michael** · 2h

Am one of the admins of the group and we have a ZERO TOLERANCE policy against the promotion of terrorist groups on this page. Please remove this post or you'll be ejected.

 **Glen** ▮▮▮▮ · 2h

ISS stands for International Space Station

 Paul ▮ · 2h

Please don't correct him, Glen 😅

 **Padraig** ▮▮▮▮▮ · 2h

International Space Station not ISIS you muppet

 **Clem** ▮▮▮▮▮ · 2h

Can't believe what I've just read. He thought Glen is promoting sighting opportunities for ISIS 😂 😂 😂 Dumbest comment I've ever seen on this page and thats saying something

 Howard ▮▮▮▮▮▮▮▮▮▮ • 1h

I think you're the one who needs to remove your post, **Michael**. You should apologise to Glen also.

Ⓜ **Michael** • 33m

Will not respond to ISS apologists. My uncle was a victim of ISS so this is a subject I know a lot about. Too many people have been hurt by the actions of ISS for me to allow ISS sympathisers to post their propaganda in this group.

 Howard ▮▮▮▮▮▮▮▮▮▮ • 12m

Actually feeling embarrassed for you. You're the one who's wrong not Glen. ISS stands for International Space Station. Proof here: https://en.wikipedia.org/International_Space_Station

Ⓠ Kira ▮▮▮▮▮▮▮ • 9m

Sorry about your uncle but you're confusing ISIS with ISS. ISIS is a terrorist organisation, ISS is the Space Station and has never harmed anyone.

(M) **Michael** · 4m

Not true. My uncle strained his neck trying to look at it when it was passing over his house last September. We cannot allow these international space terrorists to continue causing minor neck injuries to our beloved relatives.

Pat's 30th

What is the most special day of the year?
Your best friend's birthday, of course! So that's
why I always make a special effort whenever
I hear of a surprise birthday party. This is my
chance to show people how much they mean to
me. And, after all, if a stranger is just a friend
you haven't met yet, isn't every day your
best friend's birthday?

Lauren · 16 hrs

Hi all! We're having a party in the house
on Saturday October 16 to celebrate Pat's
30th birthday! If you are interested in
helping out with the preparations or just
want to keep up with whats going on,
inbox me or text me on  and I'll
ad to you the whatsapp group so we can
sort whos doing what. Thanks!

22 likes   9 comments

Pat's 30th

<Lauren added you>

[+353 ⬛⬛⬛⬛⬛]: 13:00

no probs ill be there at 3 sean says he will collect susie and the 2 girls

Michael: 13:01

Hi everyone! Thanks for adding me to the group!

Lauren: 13:02

Brilliant Sarah thanks so much!!

Lauren: 13:02

Hi Michael! Welcome to the mad House!

[+353 ⬛⬛⬛⬛⬛]: 13:04

I'll give you a call about it tomorrow Lauren but it'll be no problem at all

Michael: 13:05

OMG, I can't wait for this party! So exciting! How many people are we expecting to attend?

Lauren: 13:06

That's great thanks Em. Around 40 or 50 Michael!

Michael: 13:08

Okay, that's a little lower than I was expecting but I'll improvise. Will readjust my preparations with these new calculations in mind

Lauren: 13:09

??? LOL what preparations are you calculating?

Michael: 13:10

Will get back to you later

Michael: 16:43

Okay everyone, I've spent the last few hours working on the official plan for Pat's party. I hope you all like it

Michael: 16:43

Lauren, you and Pat will go for a 2-hour walk at exactly 5:07pm. I need Pat out of the house to give me time to set everything up.

Lauren: 16:45

Excuse me? That is so rude you are not in charge

Michael: 16:47

The party starts when you and Pat get back at 7:07pm as you will be greeted by all 50 guests (except me) standing outside the front door, performing a rap I've written called '374 Reasons Why We Love Pat' (it's a very long and complex rap that encompasses all my favourite things about Pat but I am optimistic they'll be able to learn it in 2 hours)

Michael: 16:48

Then, at the end of the rap, I will dramatically parachute in, wearing a 'Happy 30th birthday, Pat!' T-shirt (I am getting it printed tomorrow). I will then serenade Pat with a beautiful and heart-wrenching rendition of 'Happy Birthday', which I am almost certain he will love. I will then remove my T-shirt to reveal a large tattoo on my bare chest which will also say, 'Happy 30th birthday, Pat!'*

Michael: 16:49

*My only concern is that the tattooist can't fit me in until Saturday afternoon so I am hoping the bleeding will have stopped by the time the party starts.

Michael: 16:50

I am also finalising arrangements to create an ice rink in the back garden (just in case Pat and I want to go ice-skating after all the other guests have gone home).

Lauren: 16:53

How do you know Pat exactly? I assumed you were a friend of Pat but I just asked him if he knows of anyone called Michael Cunningham and he says he never heard of you

Michael: 16:55

I haven't met Pat yet but I'm looking forward to meeting him at the party. I just saw this post on Facebook earlier and wanted to join in.

<Sheila removed you>

You can't send messages to this group because you're no longer a participant.

Gatekeeper, Gatekeeper!

An interesting tidbit about me that people may not have been aware of is that I was not always a knowledgeable man of the world and a respected member of my local community. I used to be a knowledgeable boy of the world and a respected member of my local community. And in those days of youthful exuberance, I liked nothing better than taking a break from my chores by playing innumerable games. Nowadays, I often like to teach them to my online friends.

 **Edward** ▇▇▇▇▇▇▇▇ • 1d

Does anyone have ideas for games for my kids (14 13 and 10) could play during the shutdown? I don't want them being on the xbox too much and board games don't really hold their attention. Ideally something that engages their brains and that keeps them occupied for at least an hour ot two!

15 likes   36 comments

 **Michael** · 9h

Hi Edward. Think I have the perfect game. It's called 'Gatekeeper, Gatekeeper!' My uncle taught me and my brother how to play it when we were teenagers and it kept us entertained every day of the summer holidays. Very educational too. Highly recommended 👍

 **Edward** ▮▮▮▮▮▮ · 9h

Thanks for the suggestion Michael. Sounds good! How does it work?

 **Michael** · 9h

It's exactly the same as the Swedish game of Portvakt, Portvakt! except the gatekeeper is chosen by the roll of a dice instead of a coin flip 👍

 **Alexander** ▮▮▮▮▮ · 9h

Michael Christ man, this is the most unhelpful comment I ever seen someone post. You say it like we all supposed toknow what portvakt portvakt is. Who the f▮k in this town do you think ever heard of that?

Ⓜ **Michael** • 9h

Sorry, didn't mean to confuse. For those of you unfamiliar with Portvakt, Portvakt! it's basically the same game as Chase The Scoundrel except the gatekeeper and the scoundrel are on the same team 👍

Ⓐ **Alexander** ▉▉▉▉ • 9h

Aaaand you just made it more confusing. Well done 👏 🙁

Ⓐ **Edward** ▉▉▉▉ • 8h

Not familiar with either of those Michael. Can you explain how Gatekeepers works?

Ⓜ **Michael** • 5h

Gatekeepers? Gatekeepers is a very different game to Gatekeeper, Gatekeeper! In Gatekeepers, the aim is to prevent the Scoundrel from collecting all the knowledge tokens but in Gatekeeper, Gatekeeper! each player has 14 knowledge tokens at all times (except the Bridgemaster, who controls access to the Elliptical Forest, of course, who only has 13) Also, the Scoundrel is not allowed to move diagonally in Gatekeeper, Gatekeeper! 👍

Edward ▮▮▮▮▮▮ • 5h

Forget I asked

Kathy ▮▮▮▮▮ • 5h

Is anyone else following this? I'm now obsessed with Gatekeeper, Gatekeeper 😄 😄 😄

William ▮▮▮▮▮ • 5h

Me too I don't understand any of it but I love this thread so much!! Can't wait to find out why the Bridgemaster who controls access to the elliptical forest has 13 knowledge tokens instead of the usual 14!! 😄 😇

Ⓜ **Michael** • 5h

Because the Bridgemaster who controls access to the Elliptical Forest is the only player who's allowed to steal wisdom coins from the Guttersnipe

Official Rules of Gatekeeper, Gatekeeper!

Now, despite it being pretty self-explanatory, there might be a handful of people who still aren't fully clear on the rules of Gatekeeper, Gatekeeper! so here's a quick additional summary that should resolve any confusion:

a) The Gatekeeper and the Scoundrel must immediately split up once the Guttersnipe opens the Vault of Trepidation.

b) If the Vault of Trepidation remains open for more time than it takes for the Bridgemaster to perform the Scowl of Indignation, each player (except the Guttersnipe) will be deducted one adventure seed.

d) The letters c and d swap places in the event that the Icy River becomes impassable.

c) If the Scoundrel is south of the Icy River when it becomes impassable, the Guttersnipe must forfeit one wisdom coin.

e) If the Scoundrel is north of the Icy River when it becomes impassable, the Guttersnipe must forfeit one wisdom coin. (This may sound like the exact same punishment as c) but all seasoned Gatekeeper, Gatekeeper! players know that forfeiting a wisdom coin north of the Icy River is a very different prospect to forfeiting a wisdom coin south of the Icy River.)

f) For every AMPLOminute that the Gatekeeper can keep the Scoundrel from reaching the Tree of Enchanted Fury, one Jacket of Truth will become visible on the Path of Deceit.

g) If the Guttersnipe is south of the Icy River before the Bridgemaster meets the Gatekeeper in the Garden of Eternal Autumn, the game must be restarted.

h) All players must remember that 81 Crumbs of Doubt CANNOT be exchanged for a wisdom coin. You are playing Gatekeeper, Gatekeeper! not the infamous 1935 French variation Le Portier, Le Portier!

Egg Whites

Everyone seems to be baking these days. Now I don't bake or know anything about baking but I don't think that should stop me from joining in on conversations about it. It's literally putting commonly found ingredients in a hot box and waiting. I could easily do that.

 **Gemma** ▮▮▮▮▮ • 9h

Helen Depends on the recipe but I sometimes whip some egg whites when I'm stuck. Other options I've used are buttermilk or greek yoghurt (plain only) depending on the recipe and what I was able to get my hands on! Good luck!

 **Michael** • 9h

Hi Gemma. Don't mean to contradict your post but one thing you should never, ever do in baking is use egg whites as a substitute for baking powder. That's an important lesson I learned from my uncle. And before anyone tries to cast doubt on his credentials, don't bother because he used to work in a bakery.

 **Gemma** ▮▮▮▮▮ • 9h

Michael Why? I never heard that.

Claire ▮▮▮▮▮ • 8h

Same **Gemma**. How come **Michael**?

Michael • 8h

Because he needed a job and the bakery was the only place in town that was hiring at the time.

 **Claire** ▇▇▇▇ · 8h

No I mean how come you shouldn't use egg whites as a replacement for baking powder? I've done it a good few times without any problems. What's the issue with it?

 **Sam** ▇▇▇▇▇▇ · 7h

Me too Claire, am a bit doubtful about this

 **Michael** · 2h

Don't have time to go into all the details now but when he was working in the bakery, my uncle taught me a jingle that goes 'If baking powder is out of sight, don't be tempted to use egg white'

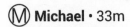 **Claire** ▇▇▇▇ · 2h

Michael Why though?

 **Michael** · 33m

I guess he just thought it would be easier for me to remember it if it rhymed and was set to a catchy melody.

Fantasy Football

Friendship isn't always about discovering
things you have in common with people.
Sometimes it's about showing people that
what they like is pointless and that there
are better things we could all be doing.

Fantasy PL 19/20

\<Dan added you\>

Liam: 18:45

Prob not. He's always been injury
prone

Dylan: 18:48

Yeah didnt realise how many games
he misses. Will replace now

Liam: 18:48

Michael: 18:50

Thanks for adding me to the group, Dan. Hi everyone! Nice to meet you all.

Dylan: 18:51

Hey Michael

James: 18:54

Welcome to the group.

You changed the subject from 'Fantasy PL 19/20' to 'Best Friends'

Best Friends

James: 18:59

?

James: 18:59

Why've you changed the name of the group?

Michael: 19:01

I didn't really like the old name. I didn't feel like it captured the true nature of the group. This name is better because it reminds us that we're best friends and that we all love each other.

James: 19:03

True nature of the group? You only just joined. Its called fantasy PL because this is a fantasy league group and it's easier to see which group is which when scrolling down

Michael: 19:04

I know but I'm not into fantasy football so that name made me feel left out.

James: 19:05

Why have you joined a fantasy football group then Einstein?

Michael: 19:07

What if we repurposed the group so that it's not about fantasy football and instead it's a place where we discuss our feelings and list all the things we love about each other? That would be better, imo.

Michael: 19:08

I'll start. I love the way James got mad at me for a second because I changed the name of the group. Classic James! 🖤 🖤 🖤

Michael: 19:09

Okay, your turn next, James. You have to say one thing you love about another member of the group! Don't be embarrassed. You're among your Best Friends! OMG, this is so much fun!

<James removed you>

You can't send messages to this group because you're no longer a participant.

Ultimate Vanquisher

If you ever see me in a supermarket buying four watermelons, you can immediately deduce one of two things: that I've decided upon a 20 per cent reduction in my daily intake of five watermelons OR that it's time for a good old-fashioned game of Ultimate Vanquisher!

 Michael · 3 hrs

Does anyone have 4 watermelons I could borrow tomorrow morning? Hoping to play a game of Ultimate Vanquisher with my brother and parents and we all have the necessary items except the watermelons for the Trial of Strength. Will maintain social distance when collecting the watermelons and I'll return them on Saturday. And for any traditionalists out there who say Ultimate Vanquisher should be played with marrows instead of watermelons, don't bother. Our family, our rules.

43 likes   19 comments

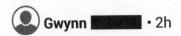 **Gwynn** ▮▮▮▮▮ • 2h

wtf have i just read?

 **Susanne** ▮▮▮▮▮▮ • 2h

Interesting.....

 **Carole** ▮▮▮▮▮ • 1h

We have a watermelon that you can have if you are near ▮▮▮▮▮ Avenue and can collect it. Maybe you can get 3 others off someone else?

 **David** ▮▮▮ • 1h

Seems I'm only one willing to ask what is this game? I don't have any water melons btw Sorry.

Ⓜ **Michael** • 52m

Ultimate Vanquisher, the game in which players face three rounds of fiendish challenges in order to be crowned Undisputed Vanquisher and receive the Jeans of Triumph. If you haven't played it, you haven't lived

 **David** ▬ • 49m

Michael I haven't lived 😔

 **Bronwyn** ▬▬▬ • 39m

Never played it never even heard of it

 **Aled** ▬▬▬▬ • 36m

Please explain the rules, Micheal. I need to know how to win the Jeans of Triumph.

Ⓜ **Michael** • 29m

I'm surprised none of you are already familiar with it but Ultimate Vanquisher is a very simple game. Four players start, three players are vanquished, two players must carry their watermelons to the nearest hazelnut tree as punishment for being vanquished and one player receives the honour of wearing the Jeans of Triumph and the knowledge that he/she is unvanquished.

 **Aled** ▬▬▬▬ · 27m

Incredible stuff. I had no idea Ultimate Vanquisher was what I needed in my life until right this minute.

 **Abbas** ▬▬▬▬ · 25m

Me either. More of this please! What are the 3 rounds? 🤣 🤣 🤣

Ⓜ **Michael** · 22m

It's very straightforward. The 3 elimination rounds are:

1. Welcome to the Vanquishing
2. The Trial of Strength
3. The Final Vanquishing

Rounds 1 and 3 are self-explanatory and the Trial of Strength involves each remaining player holding aloft a watermelon above his/her head. The player who drops his/her watermelon first is vanquished, receives the Vest of Shame and does NOT proceed to the Final Vanquishing.

 **Leanne** ▬▬▬▬▬ · 19m

If the person eliminated in round 2 gets the vest of shame what does the person eliminated in round 1 get?

 **Michael** · 18m

The Cravat of Disgrace

Abbas ▬▬▬▬▬ · 14m

 Which players have to carry their watermelons to the nearest hazelnut tree?

Michael · 7m

The players eliminated in rounds 1 and 2. The player who's eliminated in the Final Vanquishing doesn't have to do that. He/she just has to wear the Bandana of Disrepute.

Tagging on Facebook

A lot of people online feel nervous about asking a question on a public forum in case the answer is obvious and they end up looking foolish. This is not an issue for me. I ask questions online all the time. It's a great way to engage with strangers who could very soon become lifelong friends.

 Michael · 1 hr

Hi, can anyone explain how to tag people on Facebook groups? I see people doing it all the time but I think maybe my account has that option turned off? How do I turn it on? Am pretty good at computers so detailed technical explanations are fine. Thanks 👍

3 likes   39 comments

George  · 1h

It's not an option to switch on or off. Try typing @ and then the 1st letter of the name you want to type and it should come up.

Ⓜ Michael · 1h

Just tried this and it doesn't work. Don't know if you're being serious or just trying to pull the wool over my eyes but I don't like people wasting my time.

George ▮▮▮▮▮ · 1h

It does work. Here's proof: **Michael**

Ⓜ Michael · 1h

How is that proof?

George ▮▮▮▮▮ · 1h

It's proof because I just tagged you using the same way I mentioned.

Ⓜ **Michael** • 1h

> That's not proof. You might be a computer whiz and 'photo-shopped' my name into your post as a way of tricking me (which I don't appreciate, btw)

Ⓠ **George** ▓▓▓▓▓▓ • 1h

> It's a link, not an image so how can it be photoshopped? If you're on a computer, hover over it with the cursor and you'll see your profile. If you're on a phone, click it and it'll take you to your profile.

Ⓜ **Michael** • 1h

> I can't go to my profile now because I don't want to exit this thread before I know how to tag someone.

Ⓠ **George** ▓▓▓▓▓▓ • 1h

> You're not exiting a thread by clicking on a link. The thread will still be here. Are you on a phone or a computer?

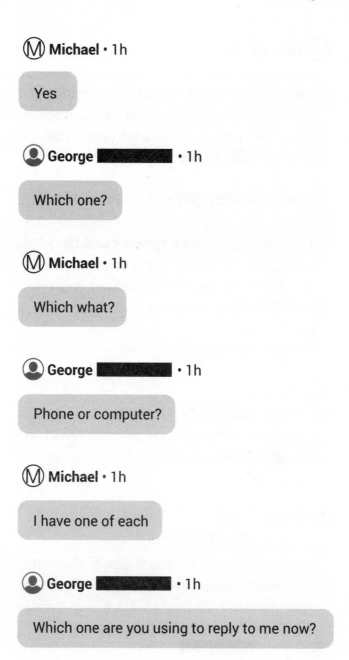

Michael · 1h

Yes

George ▮▮▮▮▮▮ · 1h

Which one?

Michael · 1h

Which what?

George ▮▮▮▮▮▮ · 1h

Phone or computer?

Michael · 1h

I have one of each

George ▮▮▮▮▮▮ · 1h

Which one are you using to reply to me now?

 **Michael** · 1h

Computer

 **George** ▮▮▮▮ · 1h

Okay so I'm going to type @ and then start spelling your name. Your name then appears and I click on it and here's what it creates: **@Michael**

 **Michael** · 1h

My name appeared!

 **George** ▮▮▮▮ · 1h

Exactly. So it does work.

 **Michael** · 59m

No because I don't want to tag myself. I want to tag someone else.

 **George** ▮▮▮▮ · 57m

I know but it works the same for everyone.

Ⓜ Michael · 54m

I'll give it a try. Thanks for your help, George.

Ⓠ George ▬▬▬▬ · 52m

You're welcome.

Ⓜ Michael · 50m

@ Dad

Ⓜ Michael · 50m

No, it doesn't work

Ⓠ George ▬▬▬ · 49m

You have to use the person's Facebook name.

Ⓜ Michael · 47m

But Dad is what I call him on Facebook

George ▮▮▮▮▮▮▮▮ • 46m

I give up.

Michael • 43m

@ Uncle Geoffrey

Michael • 43m

Still not working

Supermoon

Ever since Noel Armstring travelled to the moon on Apollo Creed 11 and then made the cowardly decision to return home immediately (instead of staying there and building a moon society), this fiery ball of mystery has been a source of fascination to mankind. Fortunately there are now experts like me to provide insight and knowledge to curious minds.

Luke ▇▇▇▇▇ · 2 hrs

Pic of the supermoon over town last night

23 likes   16 comments

 **Michael** · 54m

Nice picture, Luke, and I hope you don't mind me commenting on your post but just want to point out that taking photographs of a supermoon on a smartphone is dangerous and something that NASA actively discourages. That's something I learned from my uncle, who used to work as an astronomer 👍

 **Luke** ▆▆▆▆▆▆ · 51m

No probs Michael. Everyday's a learning day. Didn't know that

 **Michael** · 38m

Very few people do. He only worked there for a couple of months so he doesn't even mention it on his LinkedIn profile.

 **Greg** ▆▆▆▆▆▆ · 29m

Michael I think he meant about it being dangerous taking pics on a phone. How come? What risks involved?

Ⓜ **Michael** · 11m

> If you're taking photos of the moon on your phone, you're probably outdoors at night and most lion attacks happen outdoors at night so you're at an increased risk of being mauled to death by lions.

Michael Caine

It is often said (by me) that celebrities are the Roman gladiators of modern times. A lot of people have pointed out (towards me) that this is a wildly inaccurate comparison and that I don't know anything about the Roman Empire. But not knowing anything about stuff is no reason not to join in online conversations.

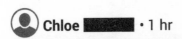 **Chloe** 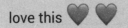 • 1 hr

love this 🤍 🤍

Michael Caine first saw Shakira Baksh on television in a coffee ad back in 1977. They have now been married for 42 years.

27 likes   29 comments 1 share

 **Michael** · 1h

Similar thing happened with my uncle but of course the media chooses to write about the celebrity instead of the common man

 **Graeme** ▰▰▰▰ · 1h

Your uncles a movie star that married a woman he saw in a coffee advert and theyre married for 42 years or are you just talking shit?

 **Michael** · 1h

I said similar, not identical

 **Shirly** ▰▰▰ · 58m

what happened Michael?

 **Michael** · 49m

Chloe posted a link to an article about Michael Caine marrying a woman he first saw on a coffee ad in 1977 and then I said something similar happened with my uncle and then Graeme seemed to cast some doubt on my claim, which I felt was unfair

Sam  • 36m

She means what happened with your uncle. What's the similar story?

Michael • 25m

Yeah, similar story except it happened in 1995 instead of 1977

Sam • 21m

He married someone from a coffee advert?

Michael • 16m

Not quite. They didn't end up getting married in the end

Shirly  • 13m

they still together?

Michael • 11m

No, they never got to meet unfortunately

Shirly ███████ • 8m

how is it supposed to be similar to the Michael Caine story?

Michael • 3m

My uncle and Michael Caine both saw a woman on a coffee ad

Tennis Partner

Wanted: Tennis Partner

Hi. I am Michael and I want to form a tennis doubles team. If you are interested, be here on Thursday at 2.38pm with your tennis equipment. I will then throw tennis balls at you for three hours from different angles to test your skills and your ability to improvise. If you succeed, I will officially name you my doubles partner and we can start entering tournaments. I have never played tennis before but I am almost certain that, with the right equimpent, I will be good at it.

Please note that you will need to provide documentation that proves you have not taken performance-enhancing drugs at any time over the last twelve years. I am not getting mixed up with a drugs cheat. If you cannot provide this proof, I will be reporting you to the tennis authorities.

Michael

Wanted: Tennis Partner (continued)

Hi. Michael again. It is now 2.39pm on Thursday and no-one showed up to be my doubles partner. I am pretty sure this is because I misspelled "equipment" in the last line of the first paragraph on my notice above. I would not want to team up with someone who makes crucial errors either. Please rest assured, though, that it was just a typo and my spelling is usually excellent.

Now that we have resolved this issue, I am happy to announce that the deadline to be my doubles partner has been extended. The new time to be here is 8.53am on Monday morning. The same rules will apply. The only difference is that you now have to bring tennis equipment for me too because I lost mine in a field.

Michael

Statistics

Statistics are used for many important purposes, such as showing karate practitioners' win/loss record and probably other stuff too. Like, I assume they're used in Statistics classes? I don't know and I don't have time to check. What I do know, however, is that statistics also feature heavily in sports. Like golf.

 Jake ▮▮▮▮▮ • 3 hrs

Serious question. Can someone tell me why the golf courses are closed? Good exercise which boosts immune system, easy to do social distancing, no risks of contamination because everyone uses their own clubs. If anyone can explain to me the problem, please let me know. When the government is lifting restrictions, golf needs to be the first one allowed back.

78 likes   41 comments

 **Michael** · 2h

Hi Jake. Here are some figures from the World Health Organisation website that I think will answer your question. Some people dispute figures for surfing but for now it's the best we've got and, as you can see, golf is in second place 👍

1. Surfing 47 12 41%
2. Golf 43 28 36%
3. Cycling 26 71 19%
4. Eagles 29 31 38%
5. Texting 31 64 31%

 **Jake** ▬▬▬ · 2h

What are these figures in relation to? What does the % of each one mean?

 **Michael** · 2h

It's a mathematical symbol, pronounced as 'per cent'. It's derived from the Latin, 'per centum', with 'per' translating as 'by' or 'for' and 'centum' meaning 'one hundred'. To put that in layman's terms, it basically means 'out of a hundred' 👍

 **Jake** ▮▮▮▮▮ · 2h

I know what percent means, I'm asking what the figures mean. What does 43 28 36% mean for golf? Are these safety calculations or what? Post a link to the full chart.

 **Euan** ▮▮▮▮▮▮ · 2h

Am I missing something or does this chart make no sense. Why are eagles in it?

Ⓜ **Michael** · 2h

Because they got 38%

 **Euan** ▮▮▮▮▮▮ · 1h

But what's the context for that? And what do the 29 and 31 mean? Without context, you've basically posted a list of random numbers.

Ⓜ **Michael** · 1h

29 and 31 are the numerical values that are used to calculate the overall percentage.

 **Euan** ▓▓▓▓▓▓▓ • 1h

An overall percentage of what?

Ⓜ **Michael** • 1h

A hundred

 **Jake** ▓▓▓▓▓ • 1h

Thanks for proving you're a moron.

 **Gabe** ▓▓▓▓▓ • 55m

This is either the stupidest or best thing I've ever read on this group. I just showed it to my wife and she asked why is cycling 3rd with 19%. I had no answer and now we're both wondering.

Ⓜ **Michael** • 53m

Because cycling only got 71 in the second column.

 **Gabe** ████████ · 49m

Michael Glad we got that cleared up

 **Euan** ████████ · 41m

Nobody knows what that 71 refers to Michael. Post the full chart.

Ⓜ **Michael** · 34m

Okay, here's the full chart.

1. Surfing 47 12 41%
2. Golf 43 28 36%
3. Cycling 26 71 19%
4. Eagles 29 31 38%
5. Texting 31 64 31%
6. Swimming (outdoors) 91 12 26%
7. Snow leopard 14 TBC 58%
8. Horses (excluding 1998-2001) 29 39 28%
9a. Wrestling 16 70 n/a
9b. Czech Republic 41 15 1001 86 42 104 61 23%
13. Joseph Stalin 34 24cm 33%

Hope that clears everything up

Joseph  • 21m

Can anyone explain what this is? Looks like gibberish to me.

Gabe  • 17m

Thanks Michael. Can't believe Czech Republic only got 23%. SMH 🌀

Henry  • 13m

Huge shock to see Snow Leopard score 58% but only finish in 7th 😕 😄

Ⓜ **Michael** • 3m

It's not finished yet. These are just the current standings but the 14 that Snow Leopard scored in the first column is certainly looking costly.

Pork Chop Recipe

When I'm online, I see a lot of people make the same mistake. They answer a question efficiently and in a manner that requires absolutely no follow-up questions. Rookie mistake. They're never going to make friends that way.

Beth  • 16 hrs

Any tips on how to cook pork chops without them turning out dry? Can't ever seem to get them right! 😂

4 likes   31 comments

 **Michael** • 16h

Hi Beth. My uncle lived in a small town in Macedonia for 3 years in the late 1980s (when it was still part of Yugoslavia) and he learned how to cook the most delicious pork chops of all time! Anyone who ever tastes them raves about them. Perfect every time! 👍

 **Beth** ▒▒▒▒▒ • 16h

Sounds tasty Michael. How does he cook them?

Ⓜ Michael • 16h

Does anyone know how to edit Facebook posts? I wrote above that my uncle lived in Macedonia for 3 years but I just texted him to confirm and he says he only lived there for 2 years. Sorry about that. Didn't mean to misinform.

Beth ▒▒▒▒▒ • 16h

Michael That's ok. What method does he use for cooking them?

Ⓜ Michael • 16h

You're probably wondering why my uncle was living in the former Yugoslavia in the late 1980s. Well, he's always been something of a linguist so he had spent much of the decade working across Europe as a translator (he speaks 6 languages). Then, in 1987, while on a walking tour of Greece, he was invited to work across the border in Macedonia. Naturally, he accepted almost immediately!

 **Beth** ████████ · 16h

What way does he cook the pork chops?

 **Michael** · 15h

Funny you should ask! Because you see, in a bizarre stroke of fortune, he ended up living next door to a local chef in Macedonia. And guess what this local chef's speciality was?

 **Beth** ████████ · 15h

Pork chops

Michael · 15h

No, spiced red cabbage

Beth ████████ · 15h

FFS

Michael · 15h

But his sister, who was also a chef, did a spectacular pork chop dish!

Beth  • 15h

Which is?

Ⓜ **Michael** • 15h

Well, my uncle and this woman became firm friends and while there was chemistry between them, neither of them was in the right place emotionally at the time to start a relationship. This is still a source of regret for my uncle as he has yet to find love. Anyway, on the day before my uncle left Macedonia, much to his surprise, she told him her secret pork chop recipe!

Beth  • 15h

FFS just say how he cooks them

Ahmed 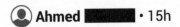 • 15h

Michael Give the recipe. Nobody wants to hear your uncles life story

Will  • 15h

Am I the only one enjoying this story?

 Beth ▰▰▰▰ · 15h

Will Yes

 Danny ▰▰ · 15h

Can't believe I've read this far down the thread and still don't know how this guy's uncle cooks pork chops.

Ⓠ Billy ▰▰▰▰ · 15h

How does he cook them Michael?

Ⓜ **Michael** · 15h

Sorry, I have no idea how my uncle cooks pork chops. He's never told anyone and he's vowed to take the recipe to his grave.

Organic Burial Pods

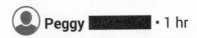 Peggy ███████ • 1 hr

Really like this idea!

'Forget Coffins – Organic Burial Pods Will Turn Your Loved Ones Into Trees'

19 likes   17 comments

 Hannah ████████ • 56m

Love this so much! Eco-friendly and still allows people to leave a physical mark on th e world. 🤍 🤍 🤍

 **Michael** · 38m

Don't believe the hype. It was a disaster when we tried this with my step-grandad

 **Hannah** ⬛⬛⬛ · 28m

Can I ask for details, Michael?

 **Michael** · 23m

My grandmother divorced my grandad in 2003 and then three years later she married a man she used to work with, who had recently become a widower. Was a little unexpected but they made each other happy

 **Hannah** ⬛⬛⬛ · 19m

Thanks for the info but I was asking for details about why the burial pod. In what way was it a disaster?

 **Michael** · 15m

The tree doesn't look like him at all

 **Hannah** ▮▮▮▮▮▮▮ • 12m

I don't know what to say to that.

 **Edward** ▮▮▮▮▮▮▮ • 6m

Right that's enough internet for me today. I'll try again tomorrow when may be there won't be someone who expected a tree to look like his dead grandad.

Ⓜ **Michael** • 1m

No, that's the problem. It DOES look like my dead grandad. Now my grandmother has a permanent reminder in her garden of her unhappy first marriage to Grandad instead of her happy second marriage to my step-grandad. If you squint, the branches look like Grandad's eyebrows, nose and ears. It upsets Nan every time she sees it.

Tennis Courts

 Tennis Courts ▶ ▬▬▬▬▬ Community · 1 hr

Here's the news we've been waiting to announe and that we hope you've been waiting to hear. As of Monday, all our courts will be reopening. We're taking bookings now and we're looking forward to seeing you!

48 likes   33 comments

 Michael · 1h

My uncle is a tennis coach but he's not on Facebook. Would appreciate if you could let him know about this. Thanks

Ann-Marie ▬▬▬▬ · 1h

Tell him yourself maybe?

 **Peter** ▮▮▮▮▮ • 56m

Michael Why can't you tell him?

Ⓜ **Michael** • 52m

Too busy. Am at work

 **Peter** ▮▮▮▮▮▮ • 49m

So why are you on Facebook?

Ⓜ **Michael** • 47m

Because I like how people post messages on my wall when it's my birthday

 **Peter** ▮▮▮▮▮ • 40m

I didn't mean why are you on Facebook in general, I was asking why are you on Facebook now if you're so busy at work?

Ⓜ **Michael** • 38m

Am on my lunch break 👍

 **Jamie** ▮▮▮▮ · 32m

Michael here's a neat idea, maybe log out off fb, and tell your uncle while you still on your break so then you don't need to ask other people to tell him, might just be crazy enough to work!!

Ⓜ **Michael** · 19m

Can't log out because I don't remember my password so wouldn't be able to log back in

 **Sammy** ▮▮▮▮▮ · 18m

Jesus christ

 ▮▮▮ **Tennis Courts** · 15m

We'd be happy to let your uncle know, **Michael**. Inbox us his number and we'll send him a text

Ⓜ **Michael** · 5m

He doesn't read his texts. Can you email him instead? His address is unclegeoffreyonline@gmail.com

▇▇▇▇▇ Tennis Courts · 1m

Done!

───────────────── Email Exchange ─────────────────

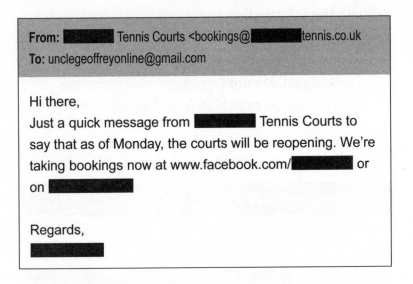

From: ▇▇▇▇▇ Tennis Courts <bookings@▇▇▇▇▇tennis.co.uk
To: unclegeoffreyonline@gmail.com

Hi there,
Just a quick message from ▇▇▇▇▇ Tennis Courts to say that as of Monday, the courts will be reopening. We're taking bookings now at www.facebook.com/▇▇▇▇▇ or on ▇▇▇▇▇

Regards,
▇▇▇▇▇

From: Uncle Geoffrey <unclegeoffreyonline@gmail.com>
To: ▇▇▇▇▇ Tennis Courts <bookings@▇▇▇▇▇tennis.co.uk

Thank you for your email. It's great news about the reopening. Looking forward to it! I must go and tell my nephew about it. He works in the shop next door to my house. He'll probably be on his lunch break now 👍

Uncle Geoffrey

Fun Run

• •

While most people you'll encounter online will be
supportive and helpful, unfortunately there is a dark
side to the information superhighway, which is that
you will sometimes meet people who go back on
their word and disrespect you and your desire
to succeed. Do not be put off. Not everyone
can be as good a friend as me.

• •

Fun Runners 8.3.20

Michael: 16:28

Hi all! Quick request. When I told
my grandmother about the 5k fun
run, she asked me to sign her up
for it and I was wondering if anyone
here would mind jogging alongside
her? Not sure how many more fun
runs she'll be able to do so I don't
want her to have to run on her own.
Thanks!

Patrick: 16:32

Judging by the way my trainings going I think I'd struggle to keep up with her 🤣 🤣 🤣

Elaine: 16:34

🩶 🩶 🩶 that's so nice Michael. Anyones welcome to join me, my partner Mark and possibly my sister. We'll be walking it. Wgat age is your gran?

Michael: 16:35

She's 87 but she's still fairly mobile. She won't be any trouble. Thanks!

Elaine: 16:36

No worries. We'll sort it out before hand!

Michael: 16:38

I'll drop her off with you 3 hours before the start time so I'll have time to familiarise myself with the route and do my warm-up exercises. Thanks again

Elaine: 16:41

Sorry are you doing the 5K too?

Michael: 16:41

Yep. Looking forward to it

Donal: 16:42

Am I missing something here? Why are you asking someone to do the 5k with your grandmother if you're doing it too?

Michael: 16:43

She's not as fast as me. My coach (a former Olimpican) advised me not to run with her because she'll only slow me down

Ciara: 16:50

Maybe make your own decision and run with her yourself?! Its a fun run. Not exactly world championships.

Donal: 16:52

Agree with Ciara. Don't ask other people to do something you should do yourself. Spend the time with your nan and enjoy it.

Elaine: 16:53

OK withdrawing offer to walk with her seen as you'll be there. Am sure she'd prefer her grandson not strangers she never met!

Michael: 16:54

Well, you already said you'd do it so you can't go back on your word

Elaine: 16:55

Yes I can. I only said yes before I knew you were doing it too

Michael: 16:56

Sorry but a deal's a deal. I shouldn't be punished just because you misunderstood

Elaine: 16:57

How are you being punished?? Running 5K with your gran isn't a punishment

Michael: 16:58

I know but losing the race because of my grandmother's frail body and poor stamina is.

Ciara: 16:58

The clue is in the name Michael. 'Fun' run. It's for fun. Run with your nan. Doesn't matter who who wins. Just enjoy it!

Michael: 17:00

LOL. Sure, I'll call my coach (the former Olimpican) and say winning doesn't matter. 'Hey Coach, it's just a fun run, lol'

Donal: 17:01

Did your Olympian coach tell you to sign up with your grandmother? Don't see many Olympians running in the same race as their nan 🤣

Michael: 17:02

It's spelt Olimpican

Donal: 17:02

No, it isn't. Look it up.

Ciara: 17:04

If winnings so important don't put your grandmother in the same race as you. Or maybe arrange a separate one where the 2 of you can run together

Michael: 17:05

I'll remember that for future races but she's already looking forward to this one and I don't want to have to lie to her that the race has been cancelled

Ciara: 17:06

Tell her the truth then. That you f██d up and want to run it on your own

Michael: 17:08

I would never say the F word to my grandmother so that's not going to work.

Ciara: 17:09

You don't have to use those exact words

Michael: 17:14

Okay, you've all been very spiteful and unhelpful so I'm withdrawing both of us from the race. Spoke with my coach (the former Olimpican) too and he advised me to leave this group chat to avoid being surrounded by toxic people. No offence.

Elaine: 17:18

How are we the toxic people? You wanted someone to mind your grandmother so you don't have too and now your calling us toxic because we said you should do it yourself. Look in the mirror instead of blaming others

Michael: 17:20

Those were my coach's words, not mine. And he's a former Olimpican so I think I'll take his word over yours

Donal: 17:21

Just FYI, Michael, it's Olympian. Spelled with a y and no c. Might help you avoid sounding like an idiot in the future.

Michael: 17:22

No, my coach used to work in The Olimpica Hotel Bar & Restaurant. They call their employees Olimpicans

<You left>

You can't send messages to this group because you're no longer a participant.

Reunion

And remember, it's always a good time to reconnect with old friends. They'll be glad to hear from you. 👍

Reunion

Hi. I am Michael and I am organising a reunion. Were you in the second carriage from the front of the 7.05am Waterford-Dublin train on February 15th, 2011? If so, be here tomorrow night at 6.17pm and we can catch up.

There were 27 of us in the carriage that day and it was a very pleasant journey. You all probably remember me. I was wearing a green coat and sitting near the back of the carriage. Sorry I haven't been in touch sooner. I have been very busy. I have karate class on Saturday mornings and piano lessons on Monday nights so that takes up a lot of my time.

Once we've caught up, we can go for something to eat. I have booked us a table at the Italian restaurant on Dame Street. I only booked it for 22 people because it would be unrealistic to expect all 27 of us to show up.

Michael

Reunion

Hi. Michael again from the poster above. I have just had an idea. After we have been to the restaurant, we could all go and get matching tattoos. I know a tattoo parlour that opens late so it wouldn't be a problem logistically. The tattoo could say, "2nd Carriage Crew 4 Life!" or something like that. We don't have to, though. It's just an idea. We can decide tomorrow.

Michael

Acknowledgements

Special thanks to my online allies and enemies who helped me to construct 'The Village' over the last five years on Twitter. Without you all joining in and adding your own creativity and weirdness, Sir Michael's world couldn't be so much fun. You're all in with an equal chance of one day winning the Prestigious Monthly Award.

Huge thanks to Carolina Larsson, who created the cover art at very short notice and had to work with my less than helpful direction of, 'It should be chaotic but also beautiful and there should be a top hat.'

And thank you to everyone who's ever DM'd me on Twitter (@Michael1979 – my door remains open) to invite me to your local community groups. I know you invited me primarily because you wanted to see me annoy your neighbours but your invitations have been a massive help.